STUDIES IN IRISH HISTORY

edited by

T. W. MOODY
Professor of Modern History, University of Dublin

R. DUDLEY EDWARDS
Professor of Modern Irish History
National University of Ireland

DAVID B. QUINN
Professor of History
University College, Swansea

VOLUME II

PROTESTANT DISSENT
IN IRELAND

1687–1780

in the same series

IRISH PUBLIC OPINION, 1750-1800
by R. B. McDowell

PROTESTANT DISSENT
IN IRELAND

1687–1780

by

J. C. BECKETT

Lecturer in History
in the Queen's University of Belfast

FABER AND FABER LTD
24 Russell Square
London

First published in mcmxlviii
by Faber and Faber Limited
24 Russell Square London W.C.1
Printed in Great Britain by
R. MacLehose and Company Limited
The University Press Glasgow
All rights reserved

PREFACE

This book is not a history of Irish protestant dissenters during the eighteenth century. So far as the presbyterians are concerned, Reid's *History of the presbyterian church in Ireland*, though first published over a century ago, covers the ground so thoroughly that there is no need to re-trace it. The other bodies of protestant dissenters, though in comparison with the presbyterians of little importance, have had their historians. But no attempt has been made to examine the whole question of protestant dissent as a problem presented to the Irish government, to the English government in so far as it was concerned with Irish affairs, to the church of Ireland and to the Irish landlords, of whom the great majority were anglicans. The following work is an attempt to analyse that problem as it existed between 1687, when James II's declaration of indulgence first held out to the protestant dissenters the prospect of a legal toleration, and 1780, when the removal of the sacramental test gave them free access to all branches of the public service.

The arrangement of the book requires some explanation. The main line of argument and the conclusions reached are laid down in the first chapter; the subsequent chapters, first in a chronological survey of the period, then in detailed examination of certain points, follow out the argument and support the conclusions. The presbyterians were the only body of protestant dissenters which was of continuous public importance throughout the period and for this reason attention has been concentrated upon their fortunes. The treatment of the minor protestant sects has concentrated in a single chapter, and this has made it possible to contrast their position with that of the presbyterians so as to clarify some of the issues involved. The legal position which the Irish presbyterians were to occupy until the removal of the sacramental test in 1780 had been settled by 1719. Consequently far more emphasis is laid on the earlier or formative part than on the later part of the period, for the basis of the relations between the government and the presbyterians remained almost unchanged throughout the middle years of the century.

Certain other points may be set down here. The term 'dissenter' when used by eighteenth-century writers always meant 'protestant dissenter', and in Ireland usually meant 'presbyterian'. In dating, the new style has been used for the years, but the days of the month have been left unaltered. All quotations have been modernized in spelling and punctuation. But in general, quotation from printed or easily accessible docu-

7

ments has been avoided where a reference to the authority for the statement made seemed sufficient.

It remains for me to express my gratitude for help received in the preparation of this book: to the officials of the various libraries and repositories in which I have worked, especially to those of the library of Trinity College, Dublin, and of the Public Record Office of Northern Ireland; to Professor T. W. Moody and Professor D. B. Quinn for guidance and advice in the collection and arrangement of material; to Professor R. Dudley Edwards for the free use of his unpublished work on the Irish protestant dissenters during the seventeenth century; to Professor J. E. Todd for the inspiration which launched me on a course of historical research, and to the Senate of the Queen's University of Belfast for a generous grant in aid of publication.

Queen's University
Belfast
February 1946

J. C. BECKETT

ABBREVIATIONS

(Full particulars of the following and of all other works cited in the footnotes are given in the bibliography.)

Bagwell, *Stuarts*	R. Bagwell, *Ireland under the Stuarts*
Cal. H. O. P.	*Calendar of home office papers*
Cal. S. P. dom.	*Calendar of state papers, domestic series*
Clarendon state letters	*State letters of Henry, earl of Clarendon . . . and his lordship's diary for the years 1687, 1688,.1689 and 1690*
Froude, *Ire.*	J. A. Froude, *The English in Ireland in the eighteenth century*
I.H.S.	*Irish Historical Studies*
King corr.	King correspondence, see note below
Lecky, *Ire.*	W. E. H. Lecky, *History of Ireland in the eighteenth century*
Liber mun. pub. Hib.	Rowley Lascelles, *Liber munerum publicorum Hiberniae*
Mant, *Ch. of Ire.*	R. Mant, *History of the church of Ireland from the revolution to the union of the churches of England and Ireland*
Phillips, *Ch. of Ire.*	W. A. Phillips (ed.), *History of the church of Ireland*
Presbyterian loyalty	[J. Fitzpatrick], *Historical essay upon the loyalty of presbyterians*
P.R.I. rep. D.K. 30	*Thirtieth report of the deputy keeper of the public records in Ireland*
P.R.N.I. rep. D.K. 1928	*Report of the deputy keeper of the records of Northern Ireland for 1928*
P.R.O.I.	Public Record Office of Ireland
P.R.O.N.I.	Public Record Office of Northern Ireland
Rec. gen. syn.	*Records of the general synod of Ulster*
Reid, *History*	J. S. Reid, *History of the presbyterian church in Ireland*, ed. W. D. Killen
Swift correspondence	*Correspondence of Jonathan Swift*, ed. F. E. Ball
T.C.D.	Library of Trinity College, Dublin
T.S.P.I.	Transcripts of state papers relating to Ireland, in the Public Record Office of Northern Ireland
Wodrow correspondence	*Correspondence of Robert Wodrow*, ed. T. McCrie

ABBREVIATIONS

Note on the King correspondence in the library of Trinity College, Dublin.

This correspondence falls into three sections distinguished in the footnotes as follows:

King corr. T.C.D.	Letters to and from King, not bound, but arranged chronologically in a series of boxes
King corr. T.C.D. (*followed by press-mark & volume*)	Letter-books containing copies of letters from King
King corr. T.C.D., transcript	Transcripts made by E. A. Phelps, late assistant librarian, T.C.D.

CONTENTS

I

INTRODUCTION: THE CASE STATED

In the interpretation of history there is a constant temptation to explain the particular by the general and to compel fact to submit to the simplifying influence of theories. The present is so obviously the result of the past that it is hard not to assume, perhaps unconsciously, the existence of a pattern of progress providing an easy explanation of the course of events. In the study of modern Irish history the danger is in some ways strengthened by the inevitable comparison with England; for when investigation has suggested a particular interpretation of some strand of English history it is obviously natural to apply the pattern to Ireland. To recognise and avoid this danger is a necessary preliminary to the present study.

One of the outstanding characteristics of modern democracy, as practised in the British commonwealth and the United States of America, is the principle of religious equality, at least in a political sense; the principle, that is, that no man should be debarred from any post for which he is otherwise qualified, merely by the profession of any particular religion, or of none at all; that, in fact, his religious opinions are entirely his own concern. Now the historian knows that this principle has developed slowly; he can point to milestones which mark the growth of religious freedom from medieval to modern times; with the removal of every privilege of an established church he sees another step taken towards the existing state of affairs. When the history of the Irish presbyterians in the eighteenth century is interpreted in this way the result is, at first sight, quite reasonable. They demanded a legal toleration, they got it; they demanded recognition for their marriages, they got it; they demanded that the sacramental test, which excluded them from public employments, should be removed, it was removed. Save for the existence of the establishment, religious equality among protestants had been almost completely secured by the end of the century. This, it may be argued, was merely an effect of the spread of eighteenth century enlightenment and religious indifferentism. But the account of the relations between the Irish presbyterians and the government which is given in the following chapters shows that the explanation is not quite so simple, and that the progress of the Irish presbyterians towards religious and political equality is not exactly parallel with the similar movement in England.

The difference arose largely from differing circumstances. Protestant

13

dissent in England was a legacy of the puritan movement, which, encouraged by its successes in the civil war and moved by the example of its Scottish allies, had overthrown episcopacy and then, finding no universally acceptable alternative, had established a sort of organised anarchy. The result was that after the restoration, the re-established church of England was faced, not by a closely-knit rival organisation, but by the scattered opposition of some hundreds of 'outed ministers', who not infrequently differed from each other as much as from the church, and whose agreement on matters of ecclesiastical establishment ended with the contention that the existing one was wrong. In Ireland, on the other hand, the distinction of protestant and papist, established at the reformation, remained virtually undisturbed till the end of the sixteenth century; and when it was upset at the beginning of the seventeenth century it was not by a native movement for further reform, but by immigration from Scotland. The Scottish settlers brought their presbyterianism with them, and for a time the new ministers established an uneasy *modus vivendi* with the bishops. But the attempt to extend the Laudian system to Ireland, the presbyterian revolt resulting from a similar attempt in Scotland, and finally the downfall of episcopacy in the civil wars, all confirmed the Ulster Scots in their presbyterian polity, pure from any admixture of the episcopal system, however modified. Thus the restored church of Ireland had to face, not the ineffectual and scattered opposition of individuals, but the concentrated and well-organised opposition of an institution whose claims were no less far-reaching than its own, and whose numerous supporters made it a powerful political force.

The significance of this distinction between protestant dissent in England and in Ireland can only be fully grasped when we consider the claims of the presbyterians. The English dissenters, however individually or locally influential, were never more than a minority; but the Irish presbyterians, at least in Ulster, claimed to be in some sort the church of the country. Race and religion with them went together. They were Scots and their church was a part of the Scottish national church. Since their immigration Ulster was, in a way, an extension of Scotland, and their church, as a self-governing extension of the church of Scotland, ought of right to enjoy the same privileges and liberties. The general synod of Ulster divided the country between sub-synods, presbyteries and congregations on a territorial basis, thus claiming a sort of general jurisdiction over the whole which aroused the anger of the established clergy. For example, when John McBride was described on the title-page of a printed sermon as 'minister of Belfast'[1] the importance of the

[1] *A sermon before the provincial synod at Antrim, preached June 1, 1698* (Belfast, 1698).

14

implication was dwelt on and driven home by the opponents of the presbyterians for years afterwards. The synod of Ulster's claim to authority did not end with the use of mere titles. Both ministers and lay people were subject to its jurisdiction, and refusal to submit might lead to a sentence of excommunication, the effect of which, in this world at least, could be very uncomfortable.

So firmly established and so well organised were the Irish presbyterians that the problem of protestant dissent could not be settled by a mere grant of toleration. From the reign of William III onwards they did, in fact, enjoy a practical toleration, at least in those places where they were already established; and their comparative indifference to the lack of toleration by statute is shown by the absence of any strong and continuous effort to secure it. The truth was that whether established by law or not, toleration could not be denied to so powerful a body. It was opposed by the high church party in the sixteen-nineties, not as wrong in itself, but because they wished to use it as a bargaining counter: toleration would be granted when the English government consented to the imposition of a sacramental test. If this test had not been imposed the presbyterians, in receipt of a government pension, enjoying a wide measure of practical toleration, with all the offices of state open to them, would have had only minor causes of grievance. But in 1704, in circumstances to be examined in a later chapter, the sacramental test was extended to Ireland, and from then onwards the main efforts of the presbyterians were concentrated on securing its repeal.

It would be wrong to regard this struggle as one for religious liberty or religious equality in a modern sense. Neither side was concerned with individuals, but with communities. The presbyterian argument in favour of removing the test was not that every man should be allowed to serve the state, irrespective of his religious convictions, but that every presbyterian should be allowed to do so, because in the past presbyterians had been instrumental in preserving the protestant and English interest, and without their help that interest would be in jeopardy. The reply to this argument was partly that presbyterian help in the past had been greatly overrated, but chiefly that the danger in accepting it now was greater than the danger in refusing it. There is nothing here about the rights of individuals and the abstract justice of universal toleration and equality on the one hand, nor about the exclusive divine right of the established church on the other. Neither side, indeed, could logically make use of such arguments. The presbyterians had no inclination to tolerate quakers, nor did they consider that the privileges which they asked for themselves should be extended to the Roman catholics, whose inveterate hostility and potential insurrection they put forward as an

15

argument in favour of their own further emancipation. On the other hand, though Swift did try to take up the attitude that no churchman who sincerely accepted the teaching of the church could wish to see the presbyterians raised to an equality,[1] yet this view could hardly be strongly held by people whose convictions were not consistent enough to prevent their accepting an unconditional toleration for the non-conforming French protestants, nor deep enough to lend any vigour to the various schemes put forward for converting the Roman catholic majority.

The best way to interpret this struggle is as one between the established church and the presbyterians over the spoils secured by the revolution—the established church in possession, the presbyterians discontented with the conduct of their former allies. The whole thing was really treated by both sides on a basis of expediency and not of principle. Though it might suit the clergy of the established church and their lay supporters from time to time to adopt the language and follow the tactics of their brethren in England they were in reality moved by very different motives; and while they might have less justification for attempting to maintain an exclusive position in the national life, they had more reason for declaring that that position was endangered by the proposal to extend toleration and equality to the protestant dissenters.

Unless this real nature of the presbyterian struggle for toleration and for repeal of the sacramental test is understood, the opposition to it is almost incomprehensible. To Froude it *was* incomprehensible; he regarded the distinction of papist and protestant as the true basis of policy in eighteenth century Ireland and anything that complicated or obliterated this plain and simple division was not only a crime but a blunder. Lecky, less concerned to pass judgement, saw in the treatment of the presbyterians merely another example of the bigotry of the established church. Ecclesiastical historians hardly penetrate further into the truth of the matter. Reid puts the presbyterian side with the vigour of a partisan rather than with the impartiality of a historian; while Mant satisfies himself with stating the church point of view as expressed by contemporaries, and makes little effort to distinguish what was just or reasonable or sincere from mere bigotry or special pleading. The result is that all four present a picture which is hard to understand. Ireland had an overwhelming Roman catholic

[1] *Queries wrote by Dr. J. Swift in the year 1732* (in *Prose works of Jonathan Swift*, ed. Temple Scott, iv. 70): 'Whether any clergymen . . . if he think his own profession most agreeable to holy scriptures, and the primitive church, can really wish in his heart, that all sectaries should be put on an equal foot with the churchmen, in the point of civil power and employments?'

16

majority, and until well on in the eighteenth century the fear of rebellion by this majority had an important if not a decisive influence on government policy. The protestant minority which, with English help, had established its ascendancy in 1690 was fairly evenly divided, as regards numbers, between presbyterians and episcopalians. During the critical years of the revolution the two had fought side by side, and both stood to lose everything if the decision of the revolution should be reversed. Common sense seemed to indicate that as co-operation had placed them in power only a continuation of that co-operation could keep them there. The presbyterian claim was that such co-operation was essential, and that it could exist only on a basis of substantial equality; this claim was rejected by the Irish church and Irish parliament. Merely to state the position in these terms, though it shows how difficult is the problem to be solved, is not in itself enough. Nor is it enough to say that the explanation is to be found in the bigotry of the high churchmen, especially when it is remembered that this opposition to the dissenters was not confined to the clergy but had the support of laymen, especially in parliament. For Irish high churchmen, with a few exceptions, were as enthusiastic as any whig or presbyterian could be for the revolution settlement, to which, they believed, they owed life, liberty and property.[1] And both in securing the triumph of William III and in preparing to face the threat to the protestant succession in 1715 they accepted the help of the presbyterians of Ulster. Bigotry, then, did not blind them to the usefulness of the presbyterians as allies, and so can hardly be put forward as a sole explanation of their unwillingness to admit them to a permanent and equal alliance with themselves against the ever-present danger from the Roman catholic majority. Some other and more reasonable principle must lie behind this seemingly incomprehensible policy. This principle may be briefly stated here, but a considerable part of the following work will be occupied in amplifying and illustrating it. First of all, when we remove from the statements of the church party the arguments which arose from mere bigotry and the arguments which they felt it expedient to use without putting any great reliance on them, it is clear that they understood more clearly than any of their historians the real nature of the struggle with the presbyterians. The latter were powerful and well organised; encouraged by the success of their brethren in Scotland and by the favour of the English government they were bound to be a danger to the privileged position of the established church. So long as their toleration was based on favour and connivance

---

[1] 'As to us here, you know we universally loved King William as our deliverer' (Bp King to Bp Ashe of Clogher, 24 Mar. 1702, in Mant, *Ch. of Ire.*, p. 125). This is typical of King's attitude.

rather than on law and so long as they were excluded from public employment, that danger was under control. Remove these checks and the danger would become active, for so long as the presbyterians were loyal to their own principles they could not remain satisfied with a subordinate position. Everything that increased their wealth and influence made them more dangerous, and took away from the power of the established church. At least during the first third of the eighteenth century (until, that is, the presbyterians were seriously weakened by internal disagreements) there was no room for a settlement of the dispute on a basis of equality, the established church could maintain its existence only by maintaining its privileged position.

But even the realisation of this state of affairs would not be sufficient to explain the policy of the high church party, if the rest of the situation were really as it has been represented; if, that is, the Irish church and government were faced with the alternatives of accepting the presbyterians as equal allies and of not having them for allies at all. No such alternatives existed, and whatever presbyterian pamphleteers said then or historians have said since, no intelligent person could be deceived about the truth of the matter. In 1689 the presbyterians did not haggle over terms before they declared for William and against James; in 1715 they did not wait for an act of indemnity before accepting commissions in the militia; and if danger were to threaten again everyone knew that either with the law or against the law they would fight for the revolution settlement.[1] The explanation, then, of the policy of the church party is simply this, that the danger of according equal treatment to the presbyterians was great and immediate, while the benefits to be derived from such concessions were, in fact, already secure.

In extension or modification of this main conclusion something must be said of the influence of the English government, which had for the Irish presbyterians something of the character of a *deus ex machina*, appearing from time to time to rescue them from the clutches of their persecutors. Why, it may be asked, was the influence of the English government not more decisive and continuous? The answer is twofold. First, the English government did not care to use, for the benefit of Irish protestant dissenters, the right which it claimed (even before 1720) of legislating for Ireland in the parliament of Great Britain.[2] Secondly,

---

[1] This was realised, at least by some observers, from the beginning. See the report of the debate on the sacramental test clause in the Irish commons, in *Cal. S. P. dom., 1703–4*, pp. 542–3.

[2] One exception was the abrogation of the oath of supremacy in Ireland by an act of the English parliament in 1691 (3 Wm & Mary c. 2).

the Irish government, especially in the early decades of the eighteenth century when the dispute over presbyterian claims was at its height, was not always amenable to English direction. The lord lieutenant, during his usually brief residence, had as his main object to get quietly through the session of parliament. In order to do this he was generally ready to bargain, and to abandon the policy which the English government had entrusted to him, on a minor point, in order to secure concessions on some matter of greater importance. Thus, though successive lord lieutenants favoured the granting of toleration and the removal of the sacramental test, and had instructions from the English government to get these measures passed, they never chose to do so at the expense of alienating powerful interests in Ireland and especially in the house of commons. It was as an alternative policy that the English government tried to make sure that the laws against the presbyterians were not strictly enforced.

Putting these two conclusions together the position may be stated, in its simplest terms, as follows. The Irish presbyterians had to deal, directly and continuously, with the Irish government, which allowed itself to be guided in its policy towards them by the views of the Irish church, and consistently refused or postponed concessions urged by the English ministry. This hostility to the presbyterians was due to fear of their influence, and was not modified by fear of the Roman catholics, against whom the presbyterians would be essential allies, because it was realised that in their own interest the latter were bound to support the established church against any attempt to overthrow the revolution settlement. Finally, the influence of the English government, though not sufficient to secure repeal of the penal laws against presbyterians, was constantly exerted to save them from the effect of those laws.

PART ONE
CHRONOLOGICAL SURVEY

‹•

II

THE PRESBYTERIANS AND THE
REVOLUTION IN IRELAND, 1687–1691

Danger, which is commonly regarded as the test of friendship, is no less certainly the test of enmity. Neighbours who in time of general security have found it impossible to live at peace will unite before the threat of common catastrophe. This is clearly exemplified in the history of Ireland during the revolutionary period. When Tyrconnell arrived as lord deputy the English element in Ireland was perfectly loyal to James,[1] was co-operating with the Roman catholics as far as the latter would allow,[2] and was displaying a bitter hostility to the protestant dissenters, and especially to the presbyterians.[3] The events of the revolution proved the hollowness alike of the alliance between churchmen and Roman catholics, and of the enmity between English and Scots.

The political history of the period is clear enough. There is no need to go over again ground which has been adequately covered by Reid and Bagwell. But for our purpose three points require elucidation: (a) the attitude of the presbyterians to the declaration of indulgence, (b) the policy and conduct of the presbyterians from November 1688 to February 1689 (i.e. from the landing of William to his acceptance as king of England), (c) the immediate effect of the revolution on the position of the presbyterians in Ireland.

1

The presbyterians and the declaration of indulgence

The most outstanding thing about the declaration of indulgence in Ireland is its comparative unimportance. In England, the declaration

[1] *Clarendon state letters*, i. 355–6.

[2] Ibid., i. 402, 406–7; ii. 8.

[3] W. King, *Answer to the considerations which compelled Peter Manby*, *as he pretends, to embrace what he calls the catholic religion* (1687), pp. 6, 29.

20

not only aroused excitement at the time, but has remained a land-mark in history. In Ireland it passed almost unnoticed.[1]

The reasons for this are to be found in the circumstances of the time. From the very beginning of James II's reign the alarm of Irish protestants of all classes had been growing. Hamilton's *Life of Bonnell* shows the alarm felt even by a non-political protestant at the trend of events quite early in the reign.[2] It was not long before the exodus of money, property and people began. Clarendon's letters bear constant witness to this.[3] The same story is told in a letter from Richard Owen to Lord Herbert of Cherbury: the papists, he says, 'are grown to such a height' that the protestants are sending their money to the new plantations, and intend to follow as soon as possible with their families.[4]

This alarm was not entirely without foundation. Clarendon arrived in Dublin in January 1686. He quickly gave orders that Roman catholics were not to be interfered with.[5] But Tyrconnell, who was the king's real representative in Ireland, soon let him know that this was not enough. The two had an interview on June 6, and two days later Clarendon sent an account of it to his brother, Rochester. After dinner, he writes, when he thought all was over, 'his lordship began a rambling discourse. . . . You must know, my lord, the king who is a Roman catholic is resolved to employ his subjects of that religion; as you will find by the letters I have brought you: and therefore some must be put out to make room for such as the king likes . . .'[6] One way in which these instructions were to be carried out was apparently by the admission of Roman catholics to corporations.[7] A month later, on July 6, Clarendon was able to report considerable progress in this task.[8]

Another point seemed to the Irish protestants even more ominous. Six months after his arrival Clarendon was visited by the Roman catholic primate, who asked if he had any instructions to pay him money.[9] The request was premature. But by September the instructions had arrived, and the payment was made. Significantly it was made out of the revenues of the vacant bishoprics of the established church.[10]

---

[1] The declaration was re-issued in Ireland on 11 Apr. 1687 (*Tudor and Stuart proclamations*, ii. no. 973).

[2] W. Hamilton, *Life of James Bonnell*, p. 39.

[3] *Clarendon state letters*, i. 222 ff., 230, 235.

[4] *Westmoreland MSS.*, p. 397.

[5] *Clarendon state letters*, i. 136.   [6] *Clarendon state letters*, i. 241 ff.

[7] Ibid., i. 280.   [8] Ibid., i. 304.   [9] Ibid., i. 260.

[10] Ibid., i. 395–6. The keeping vacant of bishoprics, deaneries etc. was as much with the object of helping the royal revenue as with that of eventually filling them with Roman catholics (Tyrconnell to lord president, 9 May 1688, in Bodl., Rawl. MS. A 139 b, f. 108, quoted in *Analecta Hibernica*, i. 38–9).

Even before this, considerable alarm had been caused by the admission of Roman catholics to the army in large numbers. In August Clarendon wrote to the king: 'That which adds to their fright is the report, which comes from considerable officers, that there will be another purge of the army after Michaelmas, and by Christmas day there shall not be an Englishman left in it'.[1]

The declaration of indulgence, then, since it gave to Roman catholics in Ireland no liberty which they did not already possess, threatened no new attack on the English interest there. That interest, in Clarendon's opinion, was loyal to the king, and quite prepared to accept the Roman catholics as equal subjects, though not to put up with the domination of the country by the natives.[2]

If the declaration could add nothing to the alarm felt by Irish protestants of the established church, one would expect the protestant dissenters to welcome it. They could not regard it as a cloak to cover the granting of liberty to Roman catholics, for that had already been done. But the presbyterians of Ulster, with whom we are here most concerned, were naturally suspicious of James. They kept in constant touch with the covenanters of Scotland[3] and saw little reason to rejoice over the king's offer. It is difficult to assess the value of the declaration to them because it is by no means clear exactly what their position was during the first years of James's reign. Reid's statement[4] that a rigorous persecution was maintained, will hardly bear investigation. The minutes of the presbytery of Antrim show that regular meetings of that presbytery were held up to March 1689. Though gaps occur in the minutes of the other presbyteries, references in those of the Antrim presbytery show that they continued to function. The evidence of these minutes is conflicting. From a query put in April 1685, it is clear that meeting-houses were then closed.[5] But at the same time the arrangements for 'supplies' show that congregations still met for worship. Later in the same year, though meeting-houses were apparently still closed, an attempt was made to start a 'philosophy school' at Antrim, and the failure of the scheme was due not to government opposition, but to the lack of students.[6] By November 1686 we learn that some ministers had gone back to their meeting-houses, apparently without opposition, and

---

[1] *Clarendon state letters*, i. 352.

[2] Ibid., i. 355, 377, 388–9.

[3] *Tudor and Stuart proclamations*, ii. no. 906.

[4] Reid, *History*, ii. 350.

[5] Minutes of the presbytery of Antrim (transcript in library of Presbyterian Historical Society, Belfast), p. 269.

[6] Ibid., pp. 273, 277.

later that those of Down had all returned.[1] At the same time, however, the presbyterians seem to have suffered from a sense of insecurity. The meeting of the presbytery at Templepatrick in June 1686, 'on serious consideration of the present affairs and hazard of liberty' decided to set up a joint committee with the presbytery of Down.[2] They seem, also, to have found it convenient to be as inconspicuous as possible. Even in May 1687 after the declaration of indulgence, they could not decide whether or not persons to be married should be publicly proclaimed, and 'scandalous persons' publicly censured. The same meeting, however, felt that the time had come for considering plans for 'planting the south of Ireland with the gospel'.[3]

All this evidence, conflicting though it is, serves to modify Reid's view. But it also indicates that there was a good deal of exaggeration in King's statement, that at the time of Tyrconnell's arrival, 'There was a free liberty of conscience by connivance, though not by law'.[4] The author of *The conduct of the dissenters* goes farther. According to him, after the defeat of the covenanters at Bothwell Bridge many Scots presbyterians took refuge in Ireland

insomuch that in the interval between the defeat of the presbyterians in Scotland and the late revolution they increased and multiplied by a numerous conflux of their brethren from Scotland; numbers of meeting-houses were built, and they were connived at in the exercise of their ecclesiastical jurisdiction, however contrary to law.[5]

But this carries back into pre-revolution days the conditions of the reign of William III. The truth seems to be that though there was a certain amount of local opposition, the presbyterians were still publicly active. In May 1686 Clarendon, writing to Archbishop Sancroft of Canterbury on the state of the Irish church, complains that the clergy neglect their cures 'which necessitates the people to look after a Romish priest or a nonconformist preacher; and there are plenty of both'.[6]

From such persecution as there was, however, the declaration of indulgence freed the presbyterians. The paucity of their thanks is not proof that there was nothing to be thankful for, though it may indicate that suspicion outweighed gratitude.[7] They seem, however, to have taken the declaration as a sign that the government was now their ally against

[1] Minutes of the presbytery of Antrim, pp. 300, 304.
[2] Ibid., p. 330.   [3] Ibid. p., 289.
[4] W. King, *State of the protestants of Ireland* (1691), p. 42.
[5] *Conduct of the dissenters*, p. 14.
[6] *Clarendon state letters*, i. 215.
[7] Reid, *History*, ii. 350–1; Bagwell, *Stuarts*, iii. 178–9.

the bishops. For example, in August 1687 it was decided to set up a committee of the various presbyteries

> to consider of several grievances arising especially from hardships by the bishops' courts and otherways, as also to consult about a commissioner, one or more, to Dublin to manage our affairs of common concernment after the said committee.

The commissioner was to be provided with a 'supplication to the lord deputy to redress the grievances mentioned by the meeting of Tyrone'.[1] Within a year this hopeful attitude had changed. In June 1688 it was decided to hold a public fast on account of 'the threatened desolation of gospel ordinances, together with present and imminent judgments'.[2]

There is another point to be noticed. The presbyterians of Ulster were very numerous, and at least in the north-east of the province formed the majority of the population.[3] Their ecclesiastical system implied not merely the right to exist but the right to dominate the country. Such a body of men, so placed, were little likely to welcome an indulgence, when they thought themselves entitled to an establishment.

2

The policy and conduct of the presbyterians from November 1688 to February 1689

Having made this bid for the support of the protestant dissenters Tyrconnell continued his task of concentrating all power in the hands of the Roman catholics. The natural result was growing alarm on the part of all the protestants of the country[4] which declarations such as that contained in the proclamation of 15 October 1688 did little to allay.[5] This fear reached panic height with the publication of the famous 'Comber letter'—an anonymous threat of a general massacre of protestants circulated during December 1688.[6] In spite of a proclamation of

[1] Minutes of the presbytery of Antrim, pp. 344–5.

[2] Ibid., pp. 411–12.

[3] According to Petty (*Political anatomy of Ireland* (1691), p. 8), the Scots presbyterians numbered 100,000, the equivalent of the 'legal protestants or conformists'. But whereas the former were concentrated in the north the latter were spread over the whole kingdom. Schomberg reported when he landed in Co. Down that the majority of the people were presbyterians (*Cal. S. P. dom, 1689–90*, p. 220). See also Bagwell, *Stuarts*, iii. 326, note.

[4] *P.R.N.I. rep. D.K. 1928*, app. A, p. 14 (extracts from letters of the earl and countess of Ardglass, written in Dec. 1688).

[5] *Tudor and Stuart proclamations*, ii. no. 1,000.

[6] King, *State of the protestants of Ireland*, app. XII.

December 7,[1] twice repeated, promising that the king would protect all his subjects without distinction of creed, this accelerated the already considerable exodus of protestants. On December 9 James Bonnell wrote: 'Last Thursday the letter threatening a massacre of all the English on this day came to town; and people not receiving such satisfaction from the lord deputy as they expected, began to think of England, and multitudes flocked away'.[2]

The attack on the corporations begun under Clarendon had also caused great alarm. In the north especially, among the presbyterians, the course of events was being carefully and anxiously watched.[3] Naturally, then, the arrival of the prince of Orange in England was welcomed as a sign of coming relief. The presbyterians of the north speedily got into touch with him.

The presbyterian ministers in the province of Ulster, with several gentlemen of note there, were the first that agreed to send an address to the prince. . . . The purport of the address . . . was . . . to represent the deplorable condition of the protestants in that kingdom and particularly in that province; and beg some speedy relief—assuring him of their readiness to serve his interest to the utmost of their power.[4]

But this must not be taken as indicating a formal renunciation of allegiance to James II, though some such interpretation was afterwards put on this action by presbyterian apologists like the author of *The loyalty of presbyterians*.[5] Tories, such as Clarendon, were already with the prince, and negotiations were in progress with the king. On December 16 Clarendon had presented to the prince 'several lords and persons of quality, English belonging to Ireland'.[6] So the northern dissenters cannot be said to have been guilty of a formal act of rebellion. At the same time, it must be noticed that the sending of their deputation coincided with outbreaks of violence, e.g. the formation of the 'Antrim association', in which presbyterians took an active if not a leading part.[7]

By the beginning of 1689 the situation had altered in two particulars. James's flight had gone far to remove the scruples of those Irish protestants who had hesitated openly to oppose the king. Tyrconnell's extensive preparations for war made the Ulster protestants acutely

[1] *Tudor and Stuart proclamations*, ii. no. 1,004.
[2] Hamilton, *Life of James Bonnell*, p. 47.
[3] J. McKenzie, *Narrative of the siege of Londonderry* (ed. Killen), ch. I.
[4] Ibid., p. 17.
[5] *An historical essay upon the loyalty of presbyterians* (Belfast, 1713), p. 395. This is usually referred to as *Presbyterian loyalty*.
[6] *Clarendon state letters*, ii. 270.
[7] McKenzie, *Narrative*, p. 63; *Presbyterian loyalty*, p. 395.

aware of their danger.[1] Already the need for armed intervention was being brought before William. On January 1 Clarendon records that the Irish protestants in London, who were very numerous, were pressing for men and arms to be sent to Ireland. The prince said 'he would take care of Ireland, as soon as things were a little settled here'. On January 4 he decided to call a meeting of the most important Irish protestants in England to discuss the situation.[2] Before any action was decided on, the Ulster protestants had taken matters into their own hands. The presbyterian ministers had sent another congratulatory address to William on January 22.[3] But the time for mere words was over. 'The lords and gentlemen of the counties of Down, Antrim, Armagh and Monaghan' were now 'associated together to stand on their defence against the Irish'. By January 25 their emissary was in London.[4] It was not long before the presbyterian ministers who had congratulated William on his arrival in England and implored his assistance for Ireland, were taking a large part in raising forces to resist King James.[5] In taking this action they were doubtless influenced by the arrival on March 9 of Captain Leighton, the emissary of the 'lords and gentlemen' mentioned above, who brought with him a letter of approval from William. This was dated February 10. But by the time the letter arrived it was known that William and Mary had been accepted as king and queen in England and they were at once proclaimed in Ulster.[6] All ambiguity in the attitude of the Ulster presbyterians was now at an end.

We can at this point attempt some general survey of their conduct and policy during these critical months. Unlike the churchmen, they were unhampered by theories of divine right or non-resistance. From the first, in spite of the declaration of indulgence, they were suspicious of James. The arrival of William in England, by giving them a potential leader and at the same time by forcing Tyrconnell to act at once, proved a turning point. The presbyterians did not immediately and openly declare for William. But this was probably due as much to the restraining influence of their new allies, the churchmen, as to any hesitation on their own part.[7] As soon as they knew that William had established himself in

[1] McKenzie, *Narrative*, p. 17.　　　　[2] *Clarendon state letters*, ii. 286, 291.

[3] McKenzie, *Narrative*, p. 17; *Presbyterian loyalty*, p. 395.

[4] *Clarendon state letters*, ii. 308.

[5] McKenzie, *Narrative*, p. 21; *Presbyterian loyalty*, p. 395. The latter stresses the close co-operation between the presbyterian ministers and 'some of the nobility and most eminent gentry of the established church'.

[6] McKenzie, *Narrative*, pp. 20, 63.

[7] In Londonderry, for example, Bishop Hopkins tried to prevent open refusal to recognise James's authority (ibid., p. 10).

England, and that he would maintain the protestant cause in Ireland, the Ulster presbyterians became his most ardent supporters.[1]

3
The position of the protestant dissenters in Ireland after the revolution

From the moment that William's success in Ireland seemed certain until the present day there have been frequent controversies about the importance of the help given to his cause by the presbyterians of Ulster. A bitter paper warfare started with Walker's *True account of the siege of Londonderry* (London, 1689) and lasted for many years. With the details of this we are not concerned, but the evidence of pamphlets on both sides confirms two conclusions which might be deduced from other sources. First, the entire interest of the dissenters, at least in the north, was solidly behind William. Secondly, while the issue was doubtful the protestants of Ireland, almost without exception, were firmly united. There was no room for distinction between churchman and dissenter while a common ruin threatened both. Each supported the other's rights. For example, when the governor of Londonderry, in July 1689, proposed terms for a cessation of arms in the north, these included not only the restoration of the privileges of the established church but also 'the full and free benefit and exercise of their religion' for all other protestants.[2] In England it was tacitly assumed that all Irish protestants had a common interest and a common policy. Sir Robert Southwell in putting forward his proposals for ending the Irish war quickly (January 1690) says the Irish protestants are 'fittest to be employed', but he seems to regard them as forming a single body.[3] Unable to deny that this unity had existed, the enemies of the dissenters later tried to make out that the latter had acted from purely selfish motives, or to minimise the extent of their aid. The author of *The conduct of the dissenters* took up the former attitude:

Upon the powerful principle of self-preservation, and that alone, did all the protestants of this kingdom unite, protect themselves and make a full stop to the progress of the Irish arms.[4]

[1] It was by no means certain from the first that William would do anything for the Irish protestants. Clarendon records (27 Feb. 1689) that many of those who had fled to England were so convinced of the uselessness of waiting for William to act that they were determined to return to Ireland if James offered reasonable terms (*Clarendon state letters*, ii. 324).

[2] McKenzie, *Narrative*, p. 69.   [3] *Cal. S. P. dom., 1689–90*, p. 440.

[4] *The conduct of the dissenters* (1712), p. 15.

Walker's argument is that the dissenters, though willing to help, played an entirely secondary role.

This unity, whatever its motive or value, did not survive the return of even partial security. *The conduct of the dissenters* lays the blame on the presbyterians, who are accused of taking advantage of the unsettled times to seize churches, attack clergy and refuse to pay tithes.[1] This, no doubt, is exaggerated; but whether or not the presbyterians took the law into their own hands after this fashion, it is clear that they did not expect their position after the war to return to what it had been even under the declaration of indulgence. But although the presbyterians had a right to expect some reward for their help, William was by no means free to choose his own method of showing his gratitude. He himself was willing to do what he could for them, but he dared not risk alienating the established church, which was jealous of its privileges and saw in every move of the Ulster presbyterians a threat not only to its ascendancy, but to its safety. The overthrow of episcopacy in Scotland must have been as alarming to the established church in Ireland as it was encouraging to the presbyterians, some of whom probably hoped for a similar settlement of the religious problem in Ulster.[2] The need for some settlement was made more urgent by the fact that Ireland was not yet by any means entirely pacified. In December 1691 an anonymous writer from Lisburn speaks of the perilous state of affairs in the north of Ireland: 'unless God's providence defends us . . . we shall all certainly perish by the Irish coming down upon us before any relief can be sent from England'.[3] The king realised that a settlement which would unite the protestant interest in loyalty to the crown would greatly strengthen his position. In November 1690 he had set up a commission in England to arrange for 'the settlement and propagation of the protestant religion in Ireland'.[4] But if it was intended thus to secure at least a legal toleration for the Irish protestant dissenters the scheme failed.

When the turmoil of war subsided the Irish presbyterians found themselves legally little better off than they had been under James II. The Irish government had done nothing for them and such immediate benefits as they derived from the revolution were due to the personal action of the king and to the English parliament. These benefits were two, the renewal of the royal grant (*regium donum*), and the abrogation,

[1] *The conduct of the dissenters*, p. 15.

[2] The whole question of the presbyterian attitude to the existing church establishment and the possibility of changing it is discussed in *Presbyterian loyalty*, pp. 404 ff.

[3] *Cal. S. P. dom., 1691-2*, p. 44.

[4] *Cal. S. P. dom., 1690-1*, pp. 155, 158-9.

by an act of the English parliament, of the oath of supremacy in Ireland. *Regium donum* was an increased resumption of a payment first made in the reign of Charles II. Though the grant was to be charged on the customs of the port of Belfast, it was made directly by the king without any reference to the Irish government. The amount was £1,200 per annum, which Sir Robert Southwell reckoned would mean £15 for every presbyterian minister in Ulster.[1]

The second concession obtained by the presbyterians at this time was the abrogation of the oath of supremacy. This oath had been imposed in 1560 (2 Eliz. cap. 2) and was obnoxious not only to Roman catholics, but also to protestant nonconformists. In 1691 an act of the English parliament (3 William and Mary, cap. 2) appointed other oaths, to which the presbyterians could not object, to be taken instead. Since the oath of supremacy was to be taken by anyone receiving royal 'fee or wage' it had excluded protestant nonconformists from the public service. The removal of the oath placed them on an equality, in that respect, with their protestant fellow-subjects.

The position, then, of the protestant dissenters of Ireland in the years immediately following the revolution was a curious one. Legally, since no toleration act had been passed, they had no right to exist at all. Yet there was no barrier to their entering the public service. Further, the presbyterians (by far the most important of the dissenting bodies) enjoyed a sort of quasi-establishment. In places where dissenting congregations were already established no attempt was made to have them removed. A considerable part of the maintenance of their ministers was provided by the state. But for all this they had no legal security. In theory they were still subject to the penalties of the acts of uniformity. The act of 1560 (2 Eliz. cap. 2) would affect nonconformists only in so far as it enforced attendance at the parish church, and this part of the act had long been a dead letter. The act of 1665 (17 and 18 Chas. II. cap. 6) was much more serious. It laid down that all schoolmasters were to receive a licence from the ordinary and that no minister who had not been episcopally ordained was to celebrate the sacrament of the Lord's supper on penalty of a fine of £100.

In seeking for a legal toleration which would repeal these acts the presbyterians were not moved by any fear of an immediate and general revival of them. They had been so long in abeyance that this would probably have proved an impossible task, even if any government had wished to undertake it. The two real grievances of which the presbyterians complained were the local and occasional persecution to which they were exposed so long as toleration was based on connivance rather

[1] *Finch MSS.*, ii. 301; *Cal. S. P. dom.*, *1690–91*, p. 481.

than law, and the inconvenience which they suffered from the action of the episcopal courts, especially in matrimonial cases. The first attempts to secure a toleration act which would redress these grievances will be dealt with in the next chapter.

III

THE STRUGGLE FOR RELIGIOUS TOLERATION DURING THE REIGN OF WILLIAM III

Disappointed of receiving immediate legal toleration as reward for their services during the revolution, the Irish presbyterians made two further attempts during the reign of William III to secure their position by an act of the Irish parliament. Though both these attempts had the sympathy of the king and of the English government, they failed, and the failure was due to the opposition of the established church in Ireland to the granting of toleration without the imposition of a sacramental test similar to that in force in England.[1] Our main problem is to discover why the Irish church refused to co-operate with the protestant dissenters, and especially with the presbyterians, in face of the dangers which threatened their common protestantism, dangers from which the revolution settlement might easily seem no more than a temporary deliverance. To any such co-operation a free legal toleration for all protestant dissenters was a necessary preliminary.

The first move was made in the Irish parliament of 1692. It was the English government which took the lead. On 2 April 1692 the earl of Nottingham sent the lords justices a list of measures to be prepared before the meeting of the Irish parliament. This list included 'a bill for the ease of protestant dissenters'.[2]

The lords justices do not appear to have been in a hurry. On July 5 Nottingham wrote to express the queen's displeasure at their delay in preparing the bills. Correspondence on the matter continued during July, and by August 1 the English government had before it a copy of 'An act for exempting their majesties' protestant subjects dissenting from the church of Ireland from the penalties of certain laws'.[3] This proposed act is mentioned again on August 25 when it is included among five which have received the queen's approval, out of seven submitted by

---

[1] The English parliament and the English government always assumed the complete unity of the 'protestant interest' in Ireland. See, e.g., the instructions issued to the lords justices, in *Cal. S. P. dom., 1693*, pp. 194–6, and to Lord Capel, ibid., *1694–5*, pp. 455–9; also address of English commons to the king, ibid., *1693*, pp. 55–6.

[2] *Cal. S. P. dom., 1691–2*, pp. 214–15.

[3] *Cal. S. P. dom., Wm III & Mary (addenda)*, p. 195.

the lords justices.[1] On the same day the lord lieutenant, Lord Sydney, arrived in Dublin,[2] and not long afterwards, on September 3, Nottingham wrote him a puzzled and rather indignant letter, from which it appears that the bills for the Irish parliament had been mislaid, and no one knew whether or not Sydney had taken them with him.[3] The bills turned up again, however, and by October 4 they were back in England. But a new difficulty was raised in a letter from Nottingham to Sydney on October 4. There was some technical irregularity in the time or method of the transmission of the bill for the protestant dissenters. This must have occurred in the earlier stages of the bill, for Nottingham attributes the fault to the lords justices, and Sydney had been sworn on September 4.[4] But since the bill was, in Nottingham's opinion, likely to be 'very useful' it should be 'sent in better form under the great seal of Ireland'.[5]

Accordingly, on October 18, Sydney informed Nottingham that the bill was being sent 'by express, under the great seal of this kingdom' to be approved in England. But in a covering letter he expresses the opinion that it will never pass the Irish parliament without the addition of a test clause.[6] Nottingham's reply, dated November 2, announces the dropping of the bill for the time being, as it would not pass without the addition of the test, which the dissenters would not like.[7] It is clear from Sydney's letter of October 18, referred to above, that the chief opposition to the bill in its original form was expected to come from the house of lords, and especially from the bishops, who usually had considerable influence there. When this parliament met there were present twelve spiritual and sixteen temporal lords. On October 10 a committee on religion was set up. This consisted of seven spiritual and nine temporal lords, but any seven were to form a quorum. On October 27 this committee presented its report. Along with the question of easing the dissenters they had considered that of maintaining the security of the established church. Though heads of a bill were to be brought in, nothing more is heard of them.[8] The commons' committee on religion, set up the day after the lords', does not seem to have reported at all.[9] The greater part of the attention of this parliament was taken up in a dispute on financial matters. Sydney, in his speech at the close of the session, 3 November 1692, complained of the attitude of the commons,

---

[1] *Cal. S. P. dom., 1691–2*, pp. 420–1.   [2] *Liber mun. pub. Hib.*, i, pt. ii, p. 9.
[3] *Cal. S. P. dom., Wm III & Mary (addenda)*, p. 198.
[4] *Liber mun. pub. Hib.*, i, pt. ii, p. 9.   [5] *Cal. S. P. dom., 1691–2*, p. 475.
[6] *Cal. S. P. dom., Wm III & Mary (addenda)*, p. 214.
[7] *Cal. S. P. dom., 1691–2*, p. 492.   [8] *Lords' jn. Ire.*, i. 447, 450, 465.
[9] *Commons' jn. Ire.*, ii. 448.

and it was probably on this account that the parliament was dissolved
by proclamation without being allowed to reassemble.[1]

Having failed in 1692, the Irish presbyterians returned to the attack
when a new Irish parliament was summoned in 1695. The occasion
seemed opportune. The lord deputy, Lord Capel, was favourable to the
dissenters and had the support of the king and of the English government for his policy.[2] The presbyterians, however, took the initiative.
They approached the English government both directly and through
their Scottish ally, Secretary Johnstone. On 19 July 1695, the latter
wrote to Shrewsbury, pressing the claims of the Irish nonconformists
to a legal toleration, and concluding with the shrewd comment that if
they could not expect it 'in the present state of affairs, they can hardly
expect it at any other time'.[3] Shrewsbury was sympathetic. He had
himself received a similar application from the Irish presbyterians. But
unless a bill was sent over by the Irish government for the purpose he
could do nothing, and so far no such bill had arrived.[4] Capel had done
his best, but the Irish privy council stood out against toleration without
a test act, and the matter had to be dropped. The leader of the opposition
to the government's policy in the council seems to have been Sir Richard
Cox, one of the judges of the King's Bench, and though the Irish
government had to abandon the bill they were able to get rid of Cox. It
was done, he says 'with great compliment'. But he goes on, 'the true
reason was, because I was a firm churchman, and stopped a bill for
"liberty of conscience", by saying I was content every man should have
liberty "of going to heaven", but I desired nobody might have liberty
of coming into government but those who would conform to it'.[5]

When parliament met Capel renewed his efforts, but with little more
success. In the house of lords permission was given to bring in heads of a
bill 'for ease to dissenters', but the matter was postponed indefinitely.[6]
In the commons, a committee set up to consider what laws in force in
England should be extended to Ireland, reported on 24 September 1695,
'that an act made in England, of the first of William and Mary, cap. 15,
entitled, An act for the ease of protestant dissenters, is fit to be made a
law in this kingdom, with such alterations as may make it practicable
in this kingdom'. But the debate which followed was adjourned and the

[1] *Commons' jn. Ire.*, ii. 485–6.
[2] Bp King to Bp Lloyd of Lichfield, 16 Dec. 1696 (Mant, *Ch. of Ire.*, p. 68).
[3] *Buccleuch & Queensbury MSS*, ii (pt I). 201.
[4] Ibid., ii. (pt I), 209–10.
[5] *Autobiography of Sir Richard Cox*, ed. Caulfield, p. 15. See also Ware,
Writers of Ireland (*Works*, ed. Harris, ii. 216).
[6] *Lords' jn. Ire.*, i. 511, 512.

matter dropped.[1] That this was due to episcopal influence is expressly claimed by King in a letter to the bishop of Lichfield (16 December 1696). 'The dissenters' interest in this kingdom is really in itself very weak and low, as sufficiently appeared in the last session of our parliament when all their interest joined with the lord deputy's, the speaker of the house of commons, and all his adherents, could not carry anything we had not a mind to . . .'[2]

The death of Lord Capel in May 1696 greatly reduced the dissenters' chance of success, and the appointment of the lord chancellor, Sir Charles Porter, as lord justice, made it almost certain that the whole affair would be abandoned. For Porter was a strong opponent of the dissenters, 'a very good friend to our church', King calls him.[3] Though Porter was not long left in sole control of the government no further attempt was made by his colleagues or successors to pass a toleration act through this parliament. All that the dissenters secured was a resolution of the house of commons, passed, apparently, without official prompting, 'that that part of the act 2 Eliz. cap. 2 . . . which obliges every person not having a lawful excuse to be absent, to resort every Sunday to church . . . ought to be put in execution against all such persons as shall not subscribe the declaration mentioned in the act of the third of William and Mary, entitled, An act for abrogating the oath of supremacy in Ireland . . . and against no other person whatsoever'.[4] This resolution, which did not even extend to formal recognition of their right to exist as organised religious bodies, shows the amount of toleration the protestant dissenters might expect from the commons.

This sharp division in the ranks of Irish protestants must at first sight appear strange, especially when we take into consideration the state of the country. The common danger that had united churchmen and dissenters, English and Scots, a few years earlier had by no means completely disappeared. In the parliament of 1695 complaints were made of the leniency shown to Roman catholics since 1690.[5] Fear of an Irish rising in the jacobite interest still remained. Such a rising would certainly follow a French invasion, in itself by no means unlikely. Sir Richard Cox mentions rumours of a French invasion in the spring of 1692.[6] The same fears remained as late as 1696.[7]

[1] *Commons' jn. Ire.*, ii. 533.   [2] Mant, *Ch. of Ire.*, p. 68.   [3] Ibid., p. 68.
[4] *Commons' jn. Ire.*, ii. 771.   [5] *Cal. S. P. dom., 1696*, p. 365.
[6] *Autobiography of Sir Richard Cox*, p. 14.
[7] Lord Capel to Shrewsbury, 7 Feb. 1696 (*Cal. S. P. dom., 1696*, p. 37). William Brewster to Sir William Turnbull, 4 Nov. 1696: 'The Irish were never so high nor the English so low'. He seems to think a plot by Irish and jacobites quite possible (*Downshire MSS*, i (pt II). 710–11).

The sense of danger was so constantly present throughout the reign that we may attribute the favour shown by the English government to this as much as to gratitude for the support given by the protestant dissenters during the revolution. When in 1699 the presbyterians tried to establish a minister in Galway, Lord Galway, then one of the lords justices, reported to the English government in terms very far from favourable to the presbyterians. He states that they were disappointed not to receive more extensive support and that they were now trying to compel the government to oppose them openly. He shows his sense of the importance of retaining their support by his declaration that this must if possible be avoided.[1] When the failure of the Darien scheme alienated many of the king's friends in Scotland the Irish presbyterians were naturally affected and even greater care was needed in dealing with them.[2] It was now that the English government had its reward for its moderate and patient policy in the assurance that even if Scotland rebelled the north of Ireland would remain quiet.[3]

But the church party in Ireland showed little either of moderation or of patience, though while the danger from Roman catholics at home and French abroad remained it might seem mere folly to drive the presbyterians also into active enmity. Nor was this opposition to toleration the work of the bishops alone: they had the backing of lay opinion. The proposal for legal toleration without a test was rejected by the commons no less than by the lords. Why did the church of Ireland, still in danger from its bitterest enemies the Roman catholics, refuse, in defiance of the pressure of the English government, to come to terms with the protestant dissenters?

Before any explanation is attempted it must be noted that this enmity was directed chiefly against the presbyterians of Ulster. Though French protestants who conformed to the established church were treated with special favour those who did not were guaranteed freedom of worship. Quakers also received special treatment from the government and from the house of commons though the bishops showed themselves less friendly.[4] The problem then becomes this, why were the supporters of the established church prepared to acquiesce in a legal toleration for

[1] Galway to Vernon, 22 Feb. 1699; 4 July 1699 (*Cal. S. P. dom., 1699–1700*, pp. 69, 234).

[2] Lord Jersey to lords justices of Ireland, 30 Jan. 1700; 6 Feb. 1700 (*Cal. S. P. dom., 1699, 1700*, pp. 368, 377).

[3] Methuen to Vernon, 20 July 1700; 1 Sept. 1700; 9 Sept. 1700 (*Cal. S. P. dom., 1700–02*, pp. 94, 115, 117).

[4] The position and treatment of protestant dissenters other than presbyterians is dealt with in Ch. XII below.

French calvinists and special legislative consideration for quakers, but not to give the sanction of law to the practical toleration which the Irish presbyterians already enjoyed?

The explanation probably is that while the minor groups of dissenters must ever rest dependent upon the tolerance of the established church the Ulster presbyterians were by their number and influence strong enough to establish an independent interest of their own. In the Irish house of commons, it is true, they counted for little; but the favour of the English government enabled them to influence affairs in Ireland.[1] It was perhaps the feeling that the English government was on their side that encouraged the presbyterians to make the most of their opportunities for strengthening their position. At any rate in the decade after the revolution various events in the north confirmed the suspicion with which churchmen and especially the bishops regarded their former allies.

Finding themselves virtually excluded from parliament the presbyterians naturally tried to get what control they could of local government. Before the end of 1691 Bishop King found himself in conflict with the corporation of Londonderry, where the dissenters were in control.[2] In 1693 they secured the appointment of one of their number as mayor. Sydney reports the matter indignantly to the earl of Nottingham. The new mayor, he says 'has never been to church in his life'.[3] Nottingham's reply, however, though professing to express the king's dissatisfaction at what had happened gives no promise of assistance, beyond suggesting that the Irish government should follow such directions 'as the law gives'.[4] But as there was no legal bar to a dissenter becoming mayor of a town, nothing could be done. In a similar case at the end of 1697 Bishop King was able to produce an episcopalian alderman who alleged a prior claim to be chosen mayor.[5] Again in 1701 the government interfered by refusing to confirm the election of a mayor on the ground that he was not a churchman.[6]

In Strabane also presbyterian influence was strong and a provost who favoured the presbyterians at the expense of the church was in office from the revolution until 1700, when an attempt was made to dislodge him, though with what success does not appear.[7]

[1] Bp King to Bp Lloyd of Lichfield, 16 Dec. 1696 (Mant, *Ch. of Ire.*, pp. 68 ff.).

[2] Bp King to Bonnell, 9 Dec. 1691 (King corr. T.C.D.).

[3] Sydney to Nottingham, 20 Feb. 1693 (*Cal. S. P. dom., 1693*, p. 39).

[4] Nottingham to Sydney, 18 Mar. 1693 (*Cal. S. P. dom., 1693*, p. 71).

[5] 'The case of Alderman Moncrieff' (King corr. T.C.D., N. 3. 1, pp. 130–2; Reid, *History*, ii. 470, 592).

[6] Bolton to Bp King, 21 Nov. 1701 (King corr. T.C.D.).

[7] Sinclair to King, 23 June 1700 (King corr. T.C.D.).

As in Londonderry so in Belfast the presbyterians made full use of the advantage they derived from numbers to get what control they could of the government of the town.[1] In this part of Ulster their position had been strengthened by the weakness of the established church. The maladministration of the absentee bishop Hackett of Down and Connor and of Archdeacon Mathews of Down had had its natural result in a great increase of dissenters.[2] So when a new bishop was appointed in 1695 Lord Capel chose a man whom he expected to get on well with the dissenters, Dr. Walkington, 'a man of great moderation and temper, which will render him more agreeable to the dissenters in the north, where his residence has been for some years past'.[3] Either Walkington was less moderate or the dissenters more unruly than Capel supposed, for it was not long before the diocese was troubled by disputes. Walkington apparently made little headway against the influence of the dissenters, and King, who had managed affairs in his own diocese of Derry with considerable success, advised him to forward a complaint to the government.[4] Presumably it was on this advice that Walkington in the same year petitioned the lords justices of England to put some check to the liberties assumed by the dissenters in his diocese.[5] The trouble arising out of a sermon preached before a presbyterian synod by John McBride, presbyterian minister of Belfast, and published in October of this year lent some colour to Walkington's complaints.[6]

Though no action seems to have followed the petition it is of great importance for its puts clearly the grounds of the fear and jealousy with which the established church regarded the presbyterians. The dissenting ministers, says Walkington, 'proceed to exercise jurisdiction openly, and with a high hand over those of their own persuasion. . . . They openly hold their sessions and provincial synods for regulating of all matters of ecclesiastical concern . . . ' This was the crux of the whole situation. The

[1] When the test act was passed the sovereign and most of the burgesses had to resign (Benn, *History of Belfast*, pp. 565, 723).

[2] Bishops of Meath and Derry to Capel, 24 Mar. 1694 (*Cal. S. P. dom., 1694–5*, p. 69). Thomas Hackett was appointed bishop of Down in 1672, but resided almost continuously in England. He was deprived in 1694 (J. C. Beckett, 'The government and the church of Ireland under William III and Anne', in *I.H.S.*, ii. 289).

[3] *Cal. S. P. dom. 1694–5*, p. 480.

[4] Bp King to Bp Walkington, 31 May 1698 (Mant, *Ch. of Ire.*, pp. 98ff). King had made an earlier offer of assistance, though without specific reference to the dissenters. Bp King to Bp Walkington, 12 June 1696 (King corr. T.C.D., N. 3. 1, p. 17).

[5] P.R.O.N.I., T. 525.

[6] — to Wodrow, 17 Oct. 1698 (P.R.O.N.I., T. 525).

presbyterians of Ulster were not a group of scattered congregations, but formed an organised body with a system of parochial, provincial and general assemblies covering the whole north of Ireland. Not only so but they were in close touch with their co-religionists in Scotland, who within a few years had been able to overthrow and persecute an established episcopal church. The parallel is too close to have been missed by either side and in proportion as it encouraged the presbyterians it must have alarmed their enemies.

This jealousy of a rival is enough to account for the clerical opposition to the proposed toleration and in some measure it would account for the opposition of the house of commons, which, except where tithes were concerned, was usually fairly favourable to the church. But the lay opposition may perhaps be further accounted for by jealousy of the growing wealth of the presbyterians, especially in the north, where, according to the author of the *Conduct of the dissenters*, they had almost completely engrossed power and trade. The decline of the woollen industry, he says, had hit the landlords, who were almost all churchmen, while the rising linen industry was almost entirely in the hands of the presbyterians.[1] It is to be noted also that an assembly of landowners like the house of commons would have little sympathy with the merchants, artisans and independent-minded farmers who composed the presbyterian community in Ulster. An example, though an extreme one, of this attitude is to be found in the policy of Sir Edward Seymour who held a large estate near Lisburn: not only did he do all he could to discourage the Scots and their religion but he even contemplated rooting them out of his estate altogether.[2]

One more point of explanation must be made. The fear of a common ruin must have forced the established church, clergy and laity alike, into an alliance with the protestant dissenters (based of course on toleration for the latter) but for this fact: the dissenters were convinced that no matter what they suffered from the ingratitude of churchmen, their position would be infinitely worse if the Roman catholics ever got the upper hand. Both church and government knew that if the protestant interest was ever threatened they could count, as in 1689–90, on the support of the protestant dissenters. The justice of this confidence was proved in 1715.[3]

Since, then, the dissenters, and especially the presbyterians, were

[1] *Conduct of the dissenters*, pp. 17, 18.

[2] Michael Harrison to Vernon, 16 July 1700 (*Cal. S. P. dom. 1700–02*, p. 93).

[3] In spite of the test act, protestant dissenters accepted commissions in the militia and acted as commissioners of array during the invasion scare of 1715 (*Commons' jn. Ire.*, iv. 255.)

bound, for their own sakes, to stand by the church in every threat to the protestant interest, the argument that toleration was necessary to secure the unity and safety of the protestants of Ireland lost most of its force. The presbyterians claimed it as a right, the English government urged it as both just and expedient, but the Irish government, convinced that it would undermine the privileges without adding to the security of the ruling class, and acting largely under the influence of the bishops, successfully opposed it as a threat to the 'existing happy constitution in church and state'.

IV

THE IMPOSITION OF THE
SACRAMENTAL TEST AND THE FIRST
ATTEMPTS TO REPEAL IT

The failure of the presbyterians to secure a toleration act was in the nature of a drawn battle; for if they did not succeed in having their legal disabilities removed, neither were their enemies in a position to enforce them strictly.

Since the abrogation of the oath of supremacy in Ireland[1] the freedom of the Irish protestant dissenters had been limited only by the terms of the acts of uniformity of 1560 and 1665.[2] The former affected protestant dissenters by making attendance at the parish church compulsory, but this was not enforced.[3] The second act of uniformity went further. By laying down that all schoolmasters must conform to the established church and have a licence from the ordinary it aimed at keeping all education under episcopal control. A more direct blow to the nonconformist ministers was the imposition of a fine of £100 on any person not episcopally ordained who administered the sacrament of the Lord's supper.[4]

In fact, however, no serious attempt was made to enforce these terms against the presbyterians of Ulster. The state of affairs in the reign of James II has already been described. After the revolution the practical toleration which they enjoyed became even more marked. Some grievances of course remained. The synod held at Antrim in 1698 complained especially of interference with presbyterian schoolmasters. This may have resulted from the activities of Bishop King earlier in the same year; for in giving instructions concerning the visitation of his diocese of Derry he wrote: 'As to the schoolmasters that keep Latin

[1] 3 Wm & Mary, c. 2 (England). This act substituted for the oath of supremacy other oaths which contained nothing offensive to protestant dissenters.

[2] 2 Eliz. c. 2; 17 & 18 Chas. II, c. 6 (Ireland).

[3] In 1697 the Irish commons expressed their approval of the non-enforcement of this part of the act against protestant dissenters (*Commons' jn. Ire.*, ii. 771).

[4] This provision was directed in the first place against ministers who tried to remain in the established church without having received episcopal ordinations; but it was also a possible weapon against the presbyterians and other nonconformist bodies (Reid, *History*, ii. 432).

schools they may be cited, and I will put them on trial according to the laws etc. And they will find that I will not let them act against the established laws'.[1] But the report made to the synod and the synod's recommendation make it clear, first, that the restrictions on schoolmasters were not general; secondly, that they were due to the action of the clergy, not to that of the government. Ministers so inconvenienced were advised to apply to a justice of the peace for assistance. Nothing could make it clearer that the government was not regarded as responsible for the persecution, but rather as an arbiter between two disputants.[2] Even while this local interference with presbyterian teachers was going on, the 'philosophy school' at Killyleagh continued to flourish without hindrance.[3] The synod did not find it necessary to repeat its complaints and presbyterian education soon became an accepted part of the life of the province, so that in 1708 it was possible to promote an act of parliament to confirm and establish a privately endowed presbyterian school.[4]

The presbyterians had, however, one serious grievance. The clergy of the established church maintained that marriages performed by presbyterian ministers were invalid, and proceedings were sometimes taken in the ecclesiastical courts to bastardise the children of such marriages and so to upset settlements made by them.[5] But though the government was approached by the bishops on the question in 1699 it seems to have taken no definite action. The presbyterian synod decided that ministers should not refuse to perform marriages, and that an address should be sent to the government asking that molestation on that account, which seems from the attitude of the synod to have been of recent origin, should be dropped.[6] The government's attitude seems to have satisfied neither side. Early in 1702 Bishop King complained to Sir Robert Southwell of the freedom with which presbyterian ministers performed the marriage ceremony; while on the other side the presbyterians sent in a long and bitter complaint in which they pointed out that this attack on them was of recent date, and that the civil courts had always recognised their marriages.[7] At this time, however, government policy seems

[1] Bp King to Dr Jenkins, 23 Apr. 1698 (King corr. T.C.D., N. 3. 1, p. 216).
[2] *Rec. gen. syn.*, i. 33.
[3] The general synod held at Antrim in June 1697 remarked on the flourishing condition of the school and resolved to support it. Ibid., i. 22.
[4] *P.R.I. rep. D.K. 30*, p. 55.
[5] Petition of Bp Walkington (P.R.O.N.I., T. 525).
[6] C. H. Irwin, *History of presbyterianism in Dublin and the south and west of Ireland*, p. 15; *Rec. gen. syn.*, i. 39.
[7] Bp King to Southwell, 28 Mar. 1702 (Mant, *Ch. of Ire.*, p. 126). 'The humble petition of the presbyterian ministers and people in the north of

to have been neutral, neither aiding nor restricting the ecclesiastical courts in the exercise of their jurisdiction.[1]

This immunity from persecution enjoyed by the Irish presbyterians during the reign of William III requires some explanation. Partly, no doubt, it was due to a sense of their services during the revolution. But probably it was due in a much larger degree to the difficulty of making persecution effective. This was caused by two things. The first was the favour shown to the Irish presbyterians by the English government, a point which has been sufficiently illustrated in the preceding chapter. It was this favour which foiled all attempts to enforce the acts of uniformity.[2] The second thing was the fact that in Ulster the presbyterians were so long and so firmly established. Though few of them were large landowners they almost monopolised trade and were very powerful on the municipal corporations.[3] So strongly entrenched was their position that on at least one occasion they even resorted to violence to secure what they considered their rights.[4] But far more solid testimony to their strength is to be found in the peaceful methods of persuasion which Bishop King adopted with them in the diocese of Derry. King was no persecutor, as his attitude to the abjuration oath shows,[5] but if he believed that the acts of uniformity could have been effectively enforced he would in all probability have made use of them. In Ulster, then, the wealth, numbers and long establishment of the presbyterians practically guaranteed them from serious persecution and the open favour of the English government gave them a sense of additional security.[6] Outside Ulster they were more open to attack, especially when they tried to establish new congregations. But even in these attempts they could count on government support at least to secure their retreat.[7]

Ireland' (P.R.O.N.I., T.525, no. 1); endorsed 'Probably *c.* 1708(?)' but attributed by Reid (*History*, ii. 484) to 1701.

[1] The whole question of marriages is dealt with in Ch. XI below.

[2] The outstanding example was at Drogheda, 1708–10. This is fully gone into with documents in Reid, *History*, iii. 3ff. See also Crosslé Papers (P.R.O.N.I., T.780, pp. 33, 47, 51); *P.R.I. rep. D.K. 30*, p. 55.

[3] *Conduct of the dissenters*, p. 17; Bp King to Southwell, 28 Mar. 1702 (Mant, *Ch. of Ire.*, p. 126).

[4] At Cookstown; Bp King to Bp Moreton of Kildare, 23 Apr. 1702 (King corr. T.C.D.).

[5] Bp King to Abp Tenison of Canterbury, 30 Nov. 1697 (King corr. T.C.D., N. 3. 1, pp. 136–7), printed in Mant, *Ch. of Ire.*, p. 78, but the date is wrongly given as 30 Oct.

[6] Bp King to Sir Robert Southwell, 28 Mar. 1702 (Mant, *Ch. of Ire.*, p. 126).

[7] As in the case of Drogheda noted above. See also Reid, *History*, ii. 523, note.

It was because the existing laws were inadequate to secure to the established church the exclusive position that its clergy thought due to it, that a section of them welcomed the sacramental test, and to some extent the abjuration oath, as new and more effective weapons against their presbyterian rivals. But though this is true there is nothing in the rather obscure history of the events leading up to the imposition of the sacramental test in Ireland to suggest that either the Irish clergy or their friends in the house of commons were responsible for the measure. When a sacramental test had been proposed previously, it had been a defensive counter to the English government's desire to grant unconditional toleration to the Irish protestant dissenters.[1] When the toleration bill was dropped nothing more was heard of the need for a test act. The proposal was suddenly revived by the English government when they added a test clause to a bill 'To prevent the further growth of popery' sent over from Ireland in 1703. This apparent change of policy on the part of the English ministry obviously required explanation. Burnet's opinion was that they had added this clause in the hope that it would cause the Irish parliament to reject the bill.[2] There is no doubt that the English government disliked many parts of the bill as it came over from Ireland,[3] and the Roman catholics exerted such influence as they could against it, influence increased by the fact that Great Britain was then in alliance with the emperor.[4] On the other hand opinion in the Irish parliament was strongly in favour of the bill, and the commons were determined to have some measure of the sort.[5] To provoke them to independent action might produce the same sort of crisis in Anglo-Irish as already existed in Anglo-Scottish relations. The unsettled state of the country increased the danger, and the prime object of the government was to get the session over quietly.[6] This would certainly explain their desire to have the objectionable popery bill rejected without bearing the responsibility for turning it down; but it does not explain why they took

[1] See Ch. III above.

[2] *History of his own times* (ed. 1753), iv. 28–9.

[3] Nottingham to lord lieutenant of Ireland, 8 July 1703 (*Cal. S. P. dom., 1703–4*, p. 43); same to same, 31 July 1703 (ibid., p. 69).

[4] Southwell to Nottingham 27 Nov. 1703 (*Cal. S. P. dom., 1703–4*, pp. 216–7); same to same, 28 Dec. 1703 (ibid., p. 248); Nottingham to Southwell, 12 Oct. 1703 (ibid., p. 151).

[5] Southwell to Nottingham 22 July 1703; same to Warre, 25 Sep. 1703; lord lieutenant to Nottingham, 10 Jan. 1704 (ibid., pp. 55, 133, 492).

[6] Ibid., pp. 54, 241–2, 243, 484. For the precarious nature of government control over the Irish commons in the early eighteenth century see J. L. McCracken, 'The conflict between the Irish administration and parliament, 1753–6', in *I.H.S.*, iii. 159–79.

this way of trying to gain their end. The number of dissenters in the Irish house of commons was negligible and to count on the churchmen rejecting a bill which they wanted for the sake of people whom they both feared and hated seems to betray an almost more than English ignorance of Irish politics. Writing on the circumstances in which the test was imposed, Archbishop Boulter says that fear of the Roman catholics 'made them willing to submit to what they did not otherwise like rather than lose their bill against popery'. This implies that the test clause was unpopular, but Boulter was writing almost thirty years after the event and his opinion must have been based on second-hand information. But his evidence for what it is worth can be used equally on the opposite side, for he adds, 'And even the dissenters then in the house begged them to take it with that clog'.[1] If the protestant dissenters themselves were willing to accept the test clause for the sake of the rest of the bill it was not likely that the churchmen would reject it to save them. Even if the English government were in any doubt before the session began, they soon had a clear warning of the attitude of the Irish commons towards the dissenters, for a month after parliament met they voted *regium donum* to be 'an unnecessary charge'.[2] So although the addition of the test clause was a surprise to most people in Ireland, the bill was never in serious danger, and when it came to a vote there were not above twenty negatives.[3] From the beginning Southwell, the Irish secretary, seemed certain that the measure would be passed, and he seems to have used all his influence to make his prophecy come true.[4] Whatever the real intentions of the English government about the bill, Southwell and the other managers of the Irish commons were apparently under the impression that it was intended to get through.

Burnet's theory, then, must be qualified; and the attempt to do so involves facing two problems. What was the attitude of the English government to the popery bill in its final form? Why was the sacramental test clause added? The first has already been touched upon. The English government did not like the bill, but under the pressure from Ireland felt obliged to give way somewhat. The result was a compromise measure, the most that England would concede, the least that Ireland would accept. This, at least, is the impression left by a study of the correspondence on the subject in the *Calendar of state papers*.[5] The second question is more difficult; and in the absence of definite evidence no

[1] Abp Boulter to Delafaye, 4 Jan. 1732 (T.S.P.I., T.722, pp. 4–5).
[2] *Cal. S. P. dom., 1703–4*, p. 164; *Commons' jn. Ire.*, iii. 62.
[3] *Cal. S. P. dom., 1703–4*, pp. 522–3, 543.
[4] Ibid., pp. 522–3, 537.
[5] See appendix to this chapter.

answer can be more than a surmise. Reid suggests that the test clause was the result of a deep scheme by high churchmen on both sides of the channel and was deliberately added at the last moment so as to weaken the chance of successful opposition by the presbyterians.[1] But this would imply a previous agreement between the English and Irish governments of which there is no evidence, indeed the addition of the test clause seems to have come as a surprise to the latter. Again, if Irish high churchmen had had anything to do with having the clause inserted, one would expect to find that Swift, who was in England at the time, was concerned in the matter. But there is nothing to show that he had any connection with it.[2] The only reasonable conclusion is that the test clause was imposed by the English government on its own initiative, without pressure from Ireland. It is very unlikely that this action arose from any hostility to protestant dissent. Though Nottingham, who was one of the most active advocates of the occasional conformity bill, did not resign until May 1704,[3] it must be remembered that he had supported the proposal for a toleration bill in Ireland in 1692. Again, though Southwell kept supplying the English government with reports, not always consistent, on the attitude of dissenters to the government, he never suggested that they required to be bridled.[4] The truth probably is that the English government were concerned more with appearance than with reality. They must produce a popery bill severe enough to satisfy the Irish commons, and at the same time persuade the emperor that responsibility for this lay in Ireland and not in England. Though the addition of a test clause was not likely to secure rejection of the bill, it was certain to provoke such a debate as would demonstrate the nature of Irish protestant opinion and prove that it was impracticable for the English government to have acted differently. Whatever the motive, or lack of motive, behind its imposition, the sacramental test came into force in Ireland in 1704,[5] and for many years the main political activities of the presbyterians were directed to securing its repeal.

When the news of the addition of the test clause arrived the presbyterians were quick to realise the danger of their position. Under Poynings' law the bill could not be amended in the Irish parliament and it was unlikely to be rejected, but they tried to get what compensation they could. Immediately after the committee stage leave was given to 'prepare and bring in heads of a bill to give such toleration to protestant

---

[1] Reid, *History*, ii. 504–5.

[2] Forster, *Life of Swift*, p. 141.

[3] *Camb. mod. hist.*, v. 464.

[4] *Cal. S. P. dom.*, *1703–4* pp. 150, 151, 229–30, 487.

[5] 2 Anne c. 6 (Ireland).

dissenters in Ireland as is by law allowed protestant dissenters in England'.[1] Early in the following year some of the leading protestant dissenters presented a petition in the house of commons setting forth the difficulty of their position under the new act.[2] Neither attempt was successful. The sacramental test was enforced, without any compensating toleration being granted. The terms were almost identical with those of the English test act (25 Car. II cap. 12). Any person holding any position, civil or military, under the crown, must not only take the customary oaths and make the usual declaration against transubstantiation, but must also, within three months of entering upon office, produce a certificate of having received the sacrament of the Lord's supper 'according to the usage of the church of Ireland . . . in some public church, upon the Lord's day commonly called Sunday, immediately after divine service and sermon'. Any office-holder who failed to comply was 'ipso facto adjudged incapable and disabled in law to all intents and purposes whatsoever to have, occupy, or enjoy the said office or offices. . . .'[3]

Though the imposition of the test was followed almost immediately by the forced resignation of Nottingham and two of his friends and the consequent strengthening of the whig element in the English government, it was some years before any effort was made on behalf of the Irish dissenters. The whigs, engaged in consolidating their position at home and pressing on the war abroad, had no time for such minor allies. It was the danger of invasion which made the condition of Ireland and the unity of all protestants there once more a matter of the first importance. By the first half of 1707 the question of repealing the test was in the air. Sir Richard Cox, then lord chancellor, attributed his dismissal in June of that year to his known opposition to any such design.[4] Opposition of this kind was widespread. The Irish parliament had not originated the test but it was prepared to defend it. The house of commons, it was said, was 'made up of two thirds as high churchmen as any in England'.[5] At the opening of the session on 7 July 1707, the lord lieutenant, the earl of Pembroke, had stressed the need for peace and security, 'and in order to the attaining of these blessings I am commanded by her Majesty to recommend to you unanimity amongst yourselves and to inform you that her majesty considering the number of papists in this realm would be glad of any expedient for the strengthening of the interest of her

[1] *Commons' jn. Ire.*, iii. 135.

[2] Ibid., iii. 212. The petition is printed in *Presbyterian loyalty*, p. 563.

[3] 2 Anne c. 6 (Ireland).

[4] *Autobiography of Sir Richard Cox*, p. 21.

[5] Reid, *History*, ii. 527.

protestant subjects in this kingdom'.[1] This was a clear hint in favour of doing something for the protestant dissenters, but the reply of the commons was vague and non-committal.[2] When, a month later, the matter was put to a trial in parliament it was quite clear that a large majority was against any tampering with the test.[3]

But the possibility of invasion still remained and in the following year the scare was at its height. The presbyterians took the opportunity of pointing out that the test deprived them of the right to serve in the militia.[4] Swift, who was in London at the time, was greatly alarmed at the effect produced by these representations, especially when they were supported by an address from the city of Dublin. In particular, he was afraid that a proposal made by the speaker of the Irish commons, that the test in Ireland should be repealed by an act of the English parliament, would be carried out. The English government, however, was apparently unwilling to do this, and tried instead to bring pressure to bear upon the churchmen in Ireland. Swift had been commissioned to secure for the Irish church a grant of the first-fruits, a concession made to the English church in 1704. It was now suggested to him that a more favourable attitude towards the repeal of the test would be the best way for the church to earn the support of government for this proposal.[5]

But by the middle of 1708 the danger of invasion seemed at an end. In July the victory of Oudenarde, followed by the possibility of an allied advance upon Paris, distracted the attention of the French government. The immediate need for conciliating the dissenters was thus removed. In February 1709 Archbishop King reported to Swift: 'I believe that matter is over for this season'.[6] By this time, however, the English cabinet had become purely whig and so could not abandon entirely the cause of religious toleration. Wharton had been appointed lord lieutenant in December 1708 and the hopes of the presbyterians were at once awakened. King speaks of 'the insolency and impudence of the dissenters on the encouragement they fancied to themselves in the change of the government here' and this, he goes on, has turned many members of parliament against them.[7] In April 1709 Wharton arrived to open a new session of parliament.[8] In his speech he stressed the need for unity

---

[1] *Commons' jn. Ire.*, iii. 271.   [2] Ibid., iii. 274.

[3] Abp King to Annesley, 16 Aug. 1707 (Mant, *Ch. of Ire.*, p. 186); Reid, *History*, ii. 526–7.

[4] *Presbyterian loyalty*, p. 478.

[5] J. C. Beckett, 'The government and the church of Ireland under William III and Anne,' in *I.H.S.*, ii. 299–300 (March 1941).

[6] Abp King to Swift, 10 Feb. 1709 (*Swift correspondence*, i. 137).

[7] Abp King to Southwell, 16 Feb. 1709 (King corr. T.C.D., transcript).

[8] *Liber mun. pub. Hib.*, i, pt. ii, p. 10.

among Irish protestants and implied that this could best be secured by some modification of the sacramental test.[1] The reply of the commons admitted the services rendered by protestant dissenters and their right to toleration, but said nothing about the test.[2] At the end of the session of 1709 and again at the opening of that of 1710 Wharton returned to the subject without achieving anything.[3] It is not clear to what extent he exceeded these general recommendations but it may be assumed that neither he nor the English government intended to push the matter too far against the wishes of the Irish parliament. Indeed before the opening of the session of 1709 the lord lieutenant's friends assured everyone of his intention to keep the 'government of state and church on the same foot as they are'.[4] Earlier still Swift had had a similar assurance from Wharton's secretary, Addison.[5] Clearly, to purchase the support of the presbyterians by alienating the established church would be a poor bargain.

Even while Wharton was trying to persuade the Irish parliament that unity among protestants was compatible with the security of the established church the position of the whigs in England was being weakened. By the end of 1710 they had been overthrown, the tories were in control and Wharton had been replaced by Ormond. For the rest of the reign the sacramental test was allowed to stand without any pressure being put on the Irish parliament to modify it.

It is hard to estimate accurately the extent to which the test affected the Irish presbyterians at this time. When rigorously enforced it drove them out of the municipal corporations. But it was not until 1707 that it was applied against the dissenting burgesses of Belfast, and apparently other corporations were not affected until later.[6] As late as 1712 there were said to be presbyterians on the common council of Dublin, though possibly the term was used in a purely political sense, to indicate

[1] Commons' jn. Ire., iii. 409.

[2] Ibid., 414–415.

[3] Ibid., 502, 514, 517–18.

[4] Abp King to Southwell, 16 Feb. 1709 (King corr. T.C.D., transcript).

[5] Swift to Abp King, London, 6 Jan. 1709 (Swift correspondence, i. 128).

[6] Benn (History of Belfast, p. 723) says that at least eight of the burgesses resigned in 1704 as a result of the test, but in November 1707 Abp King says that the act was only then being enforced in Belfast and that only four burgesses had so far complied, the rest apparently remaining in office but not acting (Mant, Ch. of Ire., p. 186). That those who had not taken the test did remain in office is clear from the resolution of the house of commons (Commons' jn. Ire., iii. 391). Doddington's opinion that this action in Belfast may mean 'purging all the corporation of Ireland' implies that some were still open to dissenters (Reid, History, ii. 528).

whigs.[1] Eventually, however, even in Antrim and Down the corporations fell completely into the hands of members of the established church, so that half a century after the repeal of the test they were still practically closed to presbyterians.[2]

Nominally the test should have excluded protestant dissenters from all paid government employment. In fact it can hardly have been interpreted in this sense. Lecky says simply, 'The presbyterians were thus expelled from all civil and military offices under the crown'.[3] But he offers no proof and enlarges no further on the subject. In spite of the act minor officials at least were probably undisturbed. This is an argument from silence rather than from positive evidence. But the silence is significant. In all the petitions, addresses and pamphlets against the test there is no mention of any general dismissal of those who did not comply and the disability about which the dissenters said most was that which they probably felt the least, exclusion from commissions in the regular army and in the militia. Writing of the militia several years after the imposition of the test Archbishop King declares, 'I do not know any officer that has on account of the test parted with his command and I do not believe there will'.[4]

But that the sacramental test was felt as a grievance is proved by the efforts made to repeal it. The demand for toleration fell into the background, all attention was concentrated on the test. English dissenters, who probably thought that repeal in Ireland would be a prelude to repeal in England, were generous in supplying money.[5] As late as the end of 1709 repeal of the test in England was considered likely.[6] While this effort was at its height the Ulster presbyterians seem to have had hopes of something more than a mere repeal of the test, even if the repeal were accompanied by a legal toleration. In 1708, writing of the state of the north of Ireland, King made this significant remark, 'Some time or another it may please God that we may push for a union and then the dissenters will be considered in course. But for them to push for an

---

[1] *P.R.I. rep. D.K. 30*, p. 53.

[2] For example, up to 1833 only one protestant dissenter had been elected a free burgess of Killyleagh. In 1834 only two of the twelve members of the corporation of Bangor were protestant dissenters. ('Report of the Irish corporation commissioners', in J. Hamilton, *Hamilton MSS*, ed. T. K. Lowry, app., p. lxxi.)

[3] Lecky, *Ire.*, i. 429. For the effect of the test upon the position of protestant dissenters in parliament, see below pp. 139-40.

[4] Abp King to Swift, 7 Apr. 1708 (*Swift correspondence*, i. 81)

[5] Swift to Abp King, 30 Nov. 1708 (*Swift correspondence*, i. 126).

[6] *Downshire MSS*, i (pt II). 868, 884.

establishment by indirect methods will hinder both us and them'.[1] But the fall of the whigs in 1710 produced such a change in the attitude of the English government as forced the dissenters both in England and in Ireland to defend the liberties they already possessed rather than seek for new ones. The last four years of Queen Anne showed the Irish presbyterians how precarious were their liberties when the influence of the English government, which since the revolution had been exerted to restrain the high church party in Ireland, could no longer be counted upon.

APPENDIX

THE passage of the sacramental test through the Irish house of commons, 1703-4.

(THE following account is extracted from *Cal. S. P. dom., 1703-4*; the page references are given at the end of each paragraph.)

On 5 June 1703 the lord lieutenant, shortly after his arrival, announced in a letter to Nottingham the formation of a committee to discuss heads of bills. This was done to give the Irish commons the idea that they had the initiative, but 'your lordship may be sure to have the same bills sent that you have already seen the heads of, but I know this way will please the people here' (p. 5).

On June 26 the lord lieutenant and Irish privy council sent to Nottingham a list of the bills which should be ready before parliament opened. This list included an 'Act to prevent the further growth of popery'. These bills were being sent in due form under the great seal of Ireland (pp. 24–5).

On July 8 Nottingham replied to the lord lieutenant, mentioning some objections to the proposed popery act (p. 43).

On July 22 Southwell wrote to Nottingham, on the lord lieutenant's behalf, admitting the possible injustices in the proposed act. But he also pointed out that the draft sent over expressed 'what is here desired', and added, 'the house here will certainly begin such a bill'. So if the English government did not like the bill in its existing form they should let it be known to what lengths they were prepared to go in such a measure (p. 55).

On July 31 Nottingham informed the lord lieutenant that certain bills were ordered to be returned. But the popery bills were being kept for reference to the attorney-general 'that he may out of them form such a bill as may be a reasonable security to the protestants and satisfactory to the people' (p. 69).

By August 8 Southwell was able to inform Nottingham that the bills which were to be sent over had reached Dublin and that arrangements were being made for parliament to be called. It was expected to meet by September 21 (p. 80).

On September 25 Southwell wrote to Richard Warre, asking what had become of the popery bill. By this time parliament had met and the commons

[1] Abp King to Oliver McCausland, 14 Oct. 1708 (King corr. T.C.D., transcript).

were resolved to have something of the sort, so it was necessary to know what would be agreed to in England (p. 133).

The attorney-general, however, was not yet finished with the bill, which he was considering along with the solicitor-general (p. 145).

On October 12 Nottingham wrote to Southwell that he had sent over a 'Bill to prevent the growth of popery'. But as it had not yet the queen's opinion it was merely sent over hastily, as a guide to what would be approved in England 'that the other measures in Ireland might be endeavoured to be prevented'. The more stringent clauses against popery were thought 'at this time not prudent while we are in alliance with princes of that religion, and especially while we are pressing particularly the emperor for favours to his protestant subjects in Hungary and Silesia' (p. 151).

On October 14 Nottingham wrote again to Southwell to tell him that no final draft of the popery bill was yet ready (p. 155).

But on October 16 the attorney-general informed Nottingham that he and the solicitor-general had the final draft ready to lay before the queen (p. 160).

On November 27 Southwell wrote to Nottingham to inform him of the adjournment of parliament. The house of commons had laid great stress on the popery bill, and had heard a rumour that the Roman catholics had made large contributions in order to oppose it (pp. 216–7).

He returned to this point in another letter to Nottingham on December 28. It was reported that the papists were soliciting hard against the popery bill, and he asked Nottingham to see that it was despatched safely (p. 248).

On 10 January 1704, on the eve of the reassembly of parliament, Southwell wrote twice to Nottingham (on his own behalf and on that of the lord lieutenant) expressing the hope that there would be as little change as possible in the popery bill, because of the great weight laid on it by the Irish commons (pp. 490–1).

Again on the same day the lord lieutenant himself wrote to Nottingham, pointing out how insistent the Irish commons were on the popery bill, and, he added, 'some gentlemen do not scruple saying that if it comes back with any material alterations, that then they will do all that can [be done] to hinder the passing of the money bill' (p. 492).

In spite of this triple appeal, on January 18 Nottingham could only write to the lord lieutenant that he thought there would be some changes in the bill, 'but I hope not such as will give any just occasion of dissatisfaction in Ireland' (p. 500).

On the same day Southwell reported to Nottingham that there was increasing feeling against Roman catholics among a section of the Irish commons, accompanied by rumours that they had risen in revolt in several parts of the kingdom. It was also being said that the popery bill would not be returned, and that the English government was very favourable towards the papists. The object of these rumours was to spread alarm and to increase distrust of the government in case the bill should be returned with any alterations (p. 501).

Parliament met again on January 20 and adjourned until January 25. Southwell reported this to Nottingham in a letter of January 22. Opposition to the government was strong, but he believed that if the main part of the popery bill came over all would be well (p. 506).

On January 26 Southwell was able to let Nottingham know that long-delayed news of their bills had reached them on the very day that parliament reassembled (January 25). He hoped that all would go well when the bills themselves arrived (p. 509).

On February 2 Nottingham informed the lord lieutenant that the queen had that day signed the warrant for the popery bill (p. 521).

By February 4 Southwell was able to send Nottingham news of how the addition of the test clause was received. Strong parties were being formed against it, but he did not think that they would be successful. It gave great satisfaction to most people with whom he had conversed (p. 522).

With his own letter Southwell enclosed one from the lord lieutenant. Both letters stressed the fact that the 'country gentlemen' were tired of being in town, and the lord lieutenant said that the government was accused of delaying matters purposely till they had gone home, 'that when the bills come back we may do what we please with them' (pp. 522–3).

On February 5 Southwell wrote to Nottingham that the bills had not yet arrived, but were impatiently expected (p. 524).

Eventually, however, the bills did arrive, the last of them on February 17. On February 19 Southwell, writing to Nottingham, expressed the hope that the session would be over in a fortnight: 'The murmur at the addition of the sacramental test abates daily, and I believe we shall hear very little of it. Tuesday we go into committee for the popery bill. At the same time the Roman catholics are to be heard *pro forma*' (p. 537).

On February 22 the popery bill was debated in the commons. The arguments of the Roman catholics were heard, but the bill was passed clause by clause, until they came to the sacramental test, upon which there was a two hours' debate: 'It was objected that this was erecting a new difference in this country between church and dissenters, when there ought only to be that of protestant and papist, that it weakened our protestant interest thereby when we were provoking the papists afresh, that it was an ill requital of the dissenters who had signalised themselves in the defence of Derry and the northern parts in the late revolution in this kingdom; that in case of any foreign invasion it put them out of capacity, without great penalty, of showing the same zeal, and that it was more sensible to the dissenters here, because they have no toleration by law as in England. And some very few in the height of their resentment were pleased to say they thought this was added on purpose to hazard the bill. All these matters were very sufficiently answered, and showed that no particular hardship was designed towards them, that in fact there was more of the church at Enniskillen, and at least one half at Derry, that even in the north above eight in ten of the gentry were churchmen, that though in those parts the commonalty might exceed in dissenters, all parish offices and duties were excused in this bill; that in cases of public danger and invasion all people were obliged both in duty and interest to oppose the common enemy, that if ever we hoped a union with England it could not be expected they would ever do it except upon the same terms that they stand upon; and that in England the dissenters have both writ for and preached conformity where it was for their interest and advantage; and as to this I must observe that the dissenters here have writ very earnestly against occasional conformity, which they now wish had been let alone' (pp. 542–3).

When the sacramental test clause was put to the vote there were not above twenty negatives. On February 25 the bill went to the house of lords, where it received a second reading (p. 543).

V

THE IRISH PRESBYTERIANS DURING THE LAST FOUR YEARS OF QUEEN ANNE

By November 1710 the tories had got complete control of the English government. Even before this the direction of Irish affairs had changed hands: in October Ormond had replaced Wharton as lord lieutenant.[1] One effect of the change was the dropping of the pressure on the Irish parliament to repeal the test. Ormond's speech at the opening of the session of 1711 contained no hint of the need for any such measure.[2] Apart from this the new English ministry made no immediate change in the treatment of the Irish protestant dissenters. No doubt the revived persecution of the non-juring presbyterians in the north was partly due to the hope of support from England, but such support was not given.[3] At the same time even moderate churchmen like Archbishop King hoped that the change of ministry would be for the good of the church, provided the clergy acted 'with temper and prudence'. In another letter he writes of the clergy: 'If they would be prudent the laity would fight their battles for them as they have done in England'.[4]

The openly expressed delight of many high churchmen at the change of ministry did not dishearten the presbyterians, and they prepared an address to the duke of Ormond.[5] They had won a substantial success at Drogheda where the government had intervened to prevent the enforcement of the act of uniformity against a presbyterian minister, though the prosecution was sponsored by the archbishop of Armagh; and this encouraged them to continue their policy of extension.[6] So far were they from feeling any need of caution that they continued to exercise ecclesiastical jurisdiction openly and in a way which was likely to attract attention.[7] Partly, perhaps, in exasperation at these activities,

---

[1] *Liber mun. pub. Hib.*, i, pt. ii, p. 10.   [2] *Commons' jn. Ire.*, iii. 600–1.

[3] An account of the Irish presbyterians and the abjuration oath is given in the next chapter.

[4] Abp King to Jenkins, 17 Feb. 1711; same to Bp Ashe of Clogher, 17 Feb. 1711 (King corr. T.C.D., N. 3. 11, pp. 316, 315).

[5] *Rec. gen. syn.*, i. 243.   [6] *P.R.I. rep. D.K. 30*, app. I, p. 55.

[7] The outstanding example was the trial by a presbyterian synod of a minister named Darragh. An account of this is given in Reid, *History*, iii.

but more probably in the hope that the new English ministry would listen sympathetically to their complaints, both the parliament and the convocation of 1711 displayed great hostility to the presbyterians. The house of lords in an address to the queen complained of the tolerant attitude of the government and pointed out the evil effects of this in the establishment of new congregations of dissenters.[1] Convocation sent up a 'Representation of the state of religion',[2] largely concerned with deism and arianism; but containing, also, such reflections upon protestant dissent as convinced Wodrow that convocation were 'like men that are for casting out presbytery in root and branch'.[3]

Though convocation, as was natural, felt it necessary to take some measures for dealing with irregular marriages[4] (a term which would include those performed by presbyterians) the main attack was directed against *regium donum*. Probably Archbishop King spoke for the majority of churchmen when he attributed all the troubles that the presbyterians were supposed to cause to this royal pension.[5] Certainly the house of lords followed his example in advocating its withdrawal, on the grounds that it had been used for the establishing of new congregations.[6] The presbyterians replied with a counter-address,[7] backed up by a deposition to the effect that the grant had been used for its intended purpose and none other.[8] They seem to have been hopeful of success,[9] and for the time their hopes were justified by the government's ignoring the suggestions of the house of lords and of convocation. So by the beginning of 1712 the activities of the Irish high churchmen, in spite of the change of government in England, had accomplished nothing against the presbyterians except against those few who refused to take

34. A letter illustrative of the hostility aroused by this assumption of judicial powers (Alexander Montgomery to ——, 22 Sep. 1711) is in Crosslé Papers (P.R.O.N.I., T.780, p. 42).

[1] *Lords' jn. Ire.*, ii. 410–11.

[2] Abp King to Swift, 10 Nov. 1711 (Mant, *Ch. of Ire.*, p. 228).

[3] Wodrow to Alexander McCracken, 27 Mar. 1712 (*Wodrow correspondence*, i. 305).

[4] The fifth of the canons passed in 1711 deals with clandestine marriages and prescribes penalties for all persons performing or attending marriages solemnized in any other form than that prescribed by the church of Ireland. See p. 119 below.

[5] Abp King to Bp Ashe of Clogher, 17 Feb. 1711 (King corr. T.C.D., N. 3. 11, p. 315).

[6] *Lords' jn. Ire.*, ii. 410–11.

[7] McCracken to [?] Wodrow, 6 Feb. 1712 (Reid, *History*, iii. 21 note).

[8] Crosslé Papers, P.R.O.N.I., T.780, p. 43.

[9] McCracken to [?] Wodrow, 6 Feb. 1712 (Reid, *History*, iii. 21 note).

the abjuration oath; even against these the persecution was fitful and its success partial.

If the presbyterians had been satisfied to wait quietly they might have escaped anything worse than the fulminations of parsons and peers. They had friends, not only in England but also among influential people in Ireland; the bishop of Clogher, for example, spoke in their favour in the parliament of 1711.[1] There was always the possibility of another change of ministry in England which would restore their friends to power. Above all, the growing fear of the pretender among all pro- testants in Ireland must have told in their favour;[2] for no matter how strongly high church an Irish landowner might be, he could not afford to be a jacobite in a country where a Stuart restoration would mean the overthrow of the existing land settlement.[3]

Unfortunately for themselves the presbyterians scarcely allowed the controversy excited by the parliament and convocation of 1711 to die down before they provided their enemies with a new ground of attack by making, rather ostentatiously, a missionary effort at Belturbet. The statements made on the one side and the other are conflicting; but the essential facts are clear enough. In December 1712 the presbytery of Monaghan met at Belturbet to establish a regular minister in that town, where there had been none before. Some gentlemen of the neighbour- hood determined to prevent this, a grand jury was empanelled and the whole presbytery was presented 'for holding an unlawful assembly, and for endeavouring to disturb the peace and union of the corporation of Belturbet'.[4] Thus the whole question of the relations between the church, the government and the presbyterians was brought to the test. As Joshua Dawson put it: 'The eyes of all people are now upon this business of Belturbet. . . .' If the government were to support the action of the jury, 'it will both stop the progress of a dangerous schism and be an encouragement to all true lovers of the English church'.[5] Petitions were sent in from both sides. The presbyterians made out their account

---

[1] *Portland MSS*, v. 20–1, 22. The bishop was St George Ashe; he was strongly anti-presbyterian on the marriage question (see below, p. 118).

[2] Abp King to Annesley, 23 Feb. 1712 (King corr. T.C.D., N. 3. 4, pt 1, p. 13); same to same, 13 Nov. 1712 (ibid., p. 65).

[3] It was on these grounds that King excused the zeal shown in Ireland against the pretender. Abp King to Bp Nicolson of Carlisle, 20 Apr. 1714 (King corr. T.C.D., N. 3. 4, pt 1, pp. 268–9).

[4] Dean Abbadie of Kilmore to Archdeacon Handcock, 17 Dec. 1712, Crosslé papers (P.R.O.N.I., T.780, p. 1).

[5] Joshua Dawson to ——, 23 Jan. 1713, Crosslé papers (P.R.O.N.I., T.780, p. 48).

of the affair.[1] The corporation petitioned in the interest of the church.[2] The dean and the vicar-general of Kilmore sent in an address in the name of the clergy of the diocese,[3] to which the bishop gave belated support from his residence in London.[4]

This Belturbet affair developed into a real trial of strength between the church and the presbyterian interest in the kingdom. The prosecution, unlike that of the non-juring ministers which was going on about the same time, was not the work of a few bigoted justices, but was given official support. A judge (Mr. Justice Coote) presided at the quarter sessions at which the indictment against the presbytery of Monaghan was presented, and he contributed largely to its success.[5] The whole ecclesiastical machinery of the diocese of Kilmore was set in motion. The lords justices, Sir Constantine Phipps and Archbishop Vesey of Tuam, in their official report complained of the conduct of the presbyterians and declared 'that if such proceedings are not discountenanced the consequence of them must be the destruction of the English church in this kingdom'.[6] Sir Constantine Phipps, in a separate letter to the lord treasurer, gave an account of the affair very unfavourable to the presbyterians, who, he said, had threatened 'to make a Drogheda of Belturbet'.[7] Now at last, it seemed, the English government would have to adopt a definite policy towards the Irish presbyterians. On the one hand, the church claimed that here was a clear case of intrusion, an attempt to set up a new congregation.[8] On the other hand, if a peaceful meeting of presbyterian ministers could be indicted for unlawful assembly, religious toleration was at an end. But the English government had no desire to declare a clear-cut policy; to do so would certainly alienate one side or the other. The exact course of the negotia-

[1] An account of the affair at Belturbet by the accused ministers (ibid. pp. 45–6). Address to lords justices of Ireland from the presbyterian ministers of the north of Ireland (ibid., p. 47). Presbyterian petition to the lord lieutenant (ibid., p. 47). Presbyterian petition to the queen (ibid., pp. 47–8).

[2] Joshua Dawson to the provost of Belturbet, 23 Dec. 1712 (ibid., p. 52).

[3] Ibid., p. 1. For an account of these addresses and counter-addresses see *P.R.I. rep. D.K. 30*, p. 55.

[4] Bp Wetenhall of Kilmore to [?] lords justices, 6 Jan. 1713 (Crosslé papers P.R.O.N.I., T.780, p. 50).

[5] Joshua Dawson to —— 23 Jan. 1713 (Crosslé papers, P.R.O.N.I., T.780, p. 48).

[6] Ibid., pp. 52–3.

[7] *Portland MSS*, v. 255.

[8] This was one of the common complaints of the churchmen in this case, e.g. letter of Phipps to the lord treasurer, mentioned above, note 3. Southwell to Dawson, 30 Dec. 1712 (Crosslé papers, P.R.O.N.I., T.780, p. 51).

tions is hard to follow, though the general result is clear enough. At first the English government postponed giving any definite answer to the letter sent by the lords justices.[1] But in the meantime they were approached from the other side. A presbyterian agent, Francis Iredell, was sent to London and got in touch with the earl of Oxford.[2] Apparently through Oxford's intervention the matter was settled by compromise; the presbyterians were allowed to have a meeting house, but it was to be a mile outside the town of Belturbet, though within the parish; the prosecution, which had been removed from the county assizes to the court of queen's bench, was to be dropped. This compromise seems to have satisfied the lords justices, though the clergy of the diocese tried to re-open the case by new protests.[3]

The whole affair, obscure as some parts of the conduct of it are, helps to show what the change of ministry meant to the Irish presbyterians. While the whigs were in power it is unlikely that the prosecution would have been begun; or if begun, it would have been quashed with less attempt at placating the established church. The Drogheda case, which was based on much firmer legal foundations (for there the persons accused had undoubtedly contravened the act of uniformity, on which ground they were indicted) was nevertheless stopped by the action of the whig ministry in England. On the other hand, the high church party in Ireland got less support than they expected, and the nature of Oxford's intervention showed that the presbyterians could still count on the influence of the English ministry to act, in some degree, as a counter-balance to the persecuting tendency of the Irish government.

In these circumstances a sort of general conflict between the church and presbyterian interests in Ireland developed out of the Belturbet dispute. The church point of view is put in a long letter, already referred to, from Sir Constantine Phipps to the lord treasurer.[4] This touches on many points of complaint, the abjuration oath,[5] the holding of synods, the attempts to interrupt the ordinary course of law, the recent intrusion at Belturbet and the arrogant conduct of the dominant presbyterian faction in Belfast. A letter from Wodrow gives the other side: 'From

[1] Southwell to Dawson, 6 Jan. 1713; 5 Feb. 1713 (ibid., p. 51).

[2] Reid, *History*, iii. 36–7. Two letters from Iredell, dealing with the Belturbet affair, but not giving the names of the recipients are in Crosslé papers, pp. 51, 67–9.

[3] The report of the lords justices on the settlement arrived at is printed in Reid, *History*, ii. 37. The terms are given in an undated letter from Iredell to an unnamed correspondent (Crosslé papers, pp. 67–9; see above, note 2).

[4] Phipps to lord treasurer, 26 Dec. 1712, *Portland MSS*, v. 254–6.

[5] See below, ch. vi.

Ireland I find our brethren there are in very ill circumstances. High church is rampant and flaming'. He goes on to refer, though not by name, to the indictment of the presbytery of Monaghan, and to other threatened dangers.[1] Many of these matters are also dealt with in a letter from Iredell to the earl of Oxford, a letter to which reference has already been made in attempting to make clear the relations between the English ministry and the Irish presbyterians.[2] As might be expected, this increase in ill-feeling caused a revival of the pamphlet war between the two parties, though, indeed, at this time it seldom ceased for long. The years 1712 and 1713 produced a notable work on each side. First came *The Conduct of the Dissenters of Ireland with respect both to Church and State* . . . (Dublin, 1712) published anonymously, but written by William Tisdal, vicar of Belfast. This is a bitter attack upon the presbyterians and makes no attempt to be impartial. But it sets out clearly the arguments by which the churchmen justified their opposition to the protestant dissenters. In 1713 came *An historical essay upon the loyalty of presbyterians* . . . . This was published without name of author, printer or place of publication; later evidence shows that it was written by James Kirkpatrick, a presbyterian minister and printed in Belfast by James Blow.[3] This work is more than a reply to Tisdal, it is a solid treatise containing much valuable historical material, including a number of letters and other documents, on which account reference has several times been made to it in previous chapters.

The conflict in which these two antagonists were engaged was concerned mainly with the questions of marriages and of *regium donum*. On the former question there had been an exchange of pamphlets between 1702 and 1705;[4] but since then it had been allowed to fall into the background and its revival in 1712 may have been in part due to convocation's action on the subject in the previous year.[5] Action was taken in the episcopal courts both against presbyterian ministers who performed the marriage ceremony and against people so married.[6] The presbyterians appealed to the lord lieutenant and to the earl of Oxford,[7] but the synod of 1714 had still to complain of the same grievance.[8] The mar-

[1] R. Wodrow to J[ohn] W[illiamson], 6 Feb. 1713 (*Wodrow correspondence*, i. 398).

[2] *Portland MSS*, v. 339–40.

[3] For details of the printing of this work see Benn, *History of Belfast*, p. 433.

[4] See below, ch. XI.

[5] See above, p. 54, n. 4.

[6] William Hair to Wodrow, 4 Dec. 1712; McBride to Wodrow, 8 Oct. 1713 (*Wodrow correspondence*, i. 484 note).

[7] McBride to Wodrow, 8 Oct. 1713 (ibid., i. 484 note).

[8] *Rec. gen. syn.*, i. 339.

riage question, however, was one with which the English government was not at this time directly concerned; so that the increase in the number of prosecutions is not to be traced to any hostility on that government's part, nor is its failure to take any action due either to hostility or to indifference. Even under a whig ministry, in 1716, the synod was still complaining of people being excommunicated for their marriages.[1]

Regium donum, on the other hand, involved the English government directly. The grant was paid out of the treasury, and the object of the church party, of moderate as well as of high churchmen, was to have it withdrawn, or at least to have the method of payment modified. The first step was to show that *regium donum* was applied by the presbyterians to uses other than those for which it was originally granted, that it enabled them to conduct schools, found new congregations, and pervert church-men. Complaints of this sort had been common enough before,[2] and the Belturbet affair both revived the anxiety of the churchmen to have *regium donum* stopped and provided them with another example of the evil results of continuing it. The lords justices in their official report declared that the money was used 'to pervert the members of the English church to schism and faction'.[3] Even before this the lords justices had decided, as a precautionary measure, to have a list drawn up of the names and residences of all the ministers to whom *regium donum* was to be paid.[4] While this scheme was being carried out, the duke of Ormond, presumably in reply to the letter of the lords justices about Belturbet, ordered them to enquire into the misapplication of *regium donum*.[5] When the list of ministers was drawn up, however, the only use made of it seems to have been to exclude three non-jurors,[6] and the advice of the lords justices was ignored. The presbyterians had grounds for the optimism expressed by Francis Iredell, '... we hope that gracious government under which we have the happiness to live will still continue her majesty's protection to those who have no other design but to serve God according to their light and conscience ...'[7]

[1] Ibid., i. 412. The history of the marriage question is dealt with consecu-tively in ch. XI.

[2] Bp King to Bp Ashe of Clogher, 24 Mar. 1702; to Sir Robert Southwell, 28 Mar. 1702 (Mant, *Ch. of Ire.*, pp. 124–5, 126–7).

[3] Crosslé papers, P.R.O.N.I., T.780, p. 53.

[4] The letter in which the lords justices announced this measure to the lord lieutenant is undated, but the demand for the list was issued before the Belturbet affair (ibid., pp. 53, 52).

[5] Ibid., p. 51.

[6] Ibid., pp. 40–1. The non-jurors here referred to were those presbyterian ministers who refused to take the abjuration oath. See ch. VI below.

[7] Ibid., p. 67.

The relief proved to be only temporary. Apparently without further pressure from Ireland and certainly without further open action by lords justices, church or parliament, *regium donum* was suspended in 1714.[1] This success of the church party in Ireland was gained after the high church Ormond had been succeeded as lord lieutenant by Shrewsbury,[2] who was supposed to be a moderate and who had appealed to Oxford that his instructions should include some relief for the presbyterians.[3] It must, therefore, be regarded as a clear indication that the tory ministry in England was coming to share the view of the Irish church and government about the treatment of protestant dissent in Ireland. The rapid growth of this similarity of outlook and policy is further seen in the proposal to extend the English schism bill to Ireland;[4] the result of it for the two factions in Ireland is seen in the almost instantaneous relief which the collapse of the English tories in August 1714 brought to the Irish presbyterians.

The events of these four years illustrate the complicated nature of the ecclesiastical administration of Ireland at the time. The Irish church and the Irish parliament each influenced, though not equally or uniformly, the government of the kingdom, especially when it was in the hands of lords justices. But this government really represented and was ultimately controlled by the English ministry. In defining relations between the Irish presbyterians and the government (which is the part of the ecclesiastical administration which here concerns us) we have to take into account all three sources of control, Irish church, Irish parliament, English ministry. The change in the last in 1710 helps us to estimate the influence of the various forces of the triangle. The only immediate difference which this change made to Irish presbyterians, and which was due to the direct action of the new ministry, was the ending of the pressure upon the Irish parliament to repeal the sacramental test. This negative policy was maintained almost to the end, and until the schism bill of 1714 no initiative in Irish ecclesiastical affairs came from England. On the other hand the new ministry did not leave the Irish church and parliament to act as they pleased. Though these two were agreed in their attitude to the presbyterians and had the support of the lords justices, they could make no fundamental alteration in government policy without the support of the English ministry. Within four years, however, partly as a result of developments in England, that support

---

[1] *Rec. gen. syn.*, i. 335, 341.

[2] *Liber mun. pub. Hib.*, i, pt ii, p. 10. Shrewsbury was appointed in September, 1713.

[3] *Portland MSS*, v. 340.

[4] See Reid, *History*, iii. 54–56.

was gained, and as the first step in a new policy *regium donum* was suspended. A comparison of the position before 1710 with the position afterwards shows that while an English whig ministry was unable to force the repeal of the sacramental test upon the Irish church and parliament the latter were able to persuade an English tory ministry to alter its religious policy. So long as the church interest in Ireland was strong enough to withstand the whigs and win over the tories it was bound to have an important, if not decisive, influence on the treatment of Irish presbyterians.

This church interest included not merely the bishops and lower clergy with their spiritual courts and, for a few years, their convocation. It meant also the Irish parliament. In the house of lords the bishops seldom formed a majority, but they usually made up almost half the house and often controlled its decisions.[1] The members of the house of commons belonged to the class most solidly devoted to the church, and in spite of quarrels with convocation over questions of privilege they were still prepared to stand by it.[2] The church itself, in the sense of an organization of clergy, probably exercised more direct influence on Irish government during the reign of Queen Anne than it had done at any time since the reformation. Early in the reign it recovered the right of meeting in convocation and so of taking a more authoritative part in ecclesiastical affairs. This success led, amongst a section of the lower clergy especially, to an excessive zeal for the assertion of privileges, which naturally increased after 1710 in the expectation of support from the new ministry.[3] The general result was a tendency to press for stricter measures against the protestant dissenters, which really meant against presbyterians. Not all the clergy agreed with this policy, at least when pressed to extremes. King, for example, writing of the schism bill, says: '... but the quaere to me is whether such laws against the dissenters etc., be the way to support the church', and he goes on to point out the need for unity among the protestants of Ireland in face of danger from the jacobites.[4] But King's opinion was not general, and in this day of

[1] During the debate in the house of lords on the bill containing the test clause (Friday 25 Feb.—Tuesday 29 Feb. 1704), attendances were as follows: spiritual peers: 25th—11, 26th—16, 28th—15, 29th—13; temporal peers:13, 14, 18, 18 (*Lords' jn. Ire.*).

[2] This loyalty continued even after the death of Anne, Abp King to Dr Charlett, 20 Apr. 1715 (Mant, *Ch. of Ire.*, p. 293).

[3] Same to same, 15 Apr. 1715 (ibid., p. 270).

[4] Abp King to Dean Story, 19 June 1714; same to Annesley, 3 July 1714 (King corr. T.C.D., N. 3. 4, pt 1, pp. 349–51, 310–11). But King was no whig. In recommending a candidate for parliament he says that he 'did not give one vote to the whigs' (ibid., p. 218).

their power the great majority of the clergy were ready to identify security with privilege, and the interests of the church with the interests of their order.

To complete this survey of the years 1710–14 it is necessary to say something of the state of affairs in which they ended. As Oxford's influence declined and that of Bolingbroke increased, the check which the English ministry imposed upon the persecuting tendency of the Irish administration became less and less effective. The church party, clergy and laity alike, were asserting their privileged position at the expense of the protestant dissenters and especially of the presbyterians. But the position was a completely unnatural one. The Irish gentry were bound in the long run to support the Hanoverian succession,[1] and it was on them that the church interest chiefly rested. Fear of the pretender was bound to increase, and in Ireland this meant fear of the Roman catholics.[2] But in any struggle with the pretender the support of the Irish presbyterians could always be counted on, and was indeed indispensable: whether churchmen recognized it or not there actually existed a basic unity between the two main divisions of Irish protestants.[3] This had not been enough to secure legal toleration for protestant dissenters, but it was enough to make the situation which had been created by the summer of 1714 an impossible one. The sacramental test gave the church security. Further persecution of the presbyterians in the long run damaged this security by dividing more deeply the protestant interest. Something of this was realized in 1715–16; but in the meantime the whig triumph of 1714 altered the state of affairs. The likelihood of any reassembly of convocation, in abeyance since 1711, almost vanished, and with convocation went the church's power of expressing its corporate opinion. The discontinuance of convocation, too, by depriving the lower clergy of a voice in the affairs of the church increased the power of the bishops, and the bishops knew that their chances of promotion depended upon the favour of the English ministry. At the same time, the independence of the Irish parliament was being curbed in the constitutional struggle which ended in the 'Sixth of

[1] See above, p. 55. The bulk of the Irish protestant landlords held their estates under the land settlement of the restoration, which was confirmed at the revolution (see King, *State of the protestants*, pp. 142 ff.).

[2] For example, in the spring of 1714, proclamations were issued against Roman catholics carrying arms (Crosslé papers, P.R.O.N.I., T.780, p. 74).

[3] '... But certainly the elector ... cannot but take pleasure that so great a body of people, as the presbyterians here and in Ireland are, will adventure their all for him against the pretender's attempts.' J—— B—— to Thomas Gordon, Edinburgh, 11 Feb. 1714 (*Portland MSS*, v. 382).

George I'. As a result of these processes the influence of the Irish church and of the Irish parliament on the ecclesiastical policy of the government rapidly declined and the control of the English ministry became more direct and continuous. From 1714 onwards the position of the Irish presbyterians depended more than ever on the attitude of the English ministry. The church interest could do nothing more than carry on a losing fight for the maintenance of the test. The means by which the church managed to retain under a long whig supremacy some of the privileged position it had gained under the tories will be discussed later.

VI

THE IRISH PRESBYTERIANS
AND THE ABJURATION OATH

In spite of much experience to the contrary, statesmen of the seventeenth and eighteenth centuries had great confidence in the efficacy of political oaths. So it was not unnatural that the supporters of William III were anxious that those who had violated their allegiance to James II should bind themselves by new and stronger ties to his successor. It was, however, only in the last year of the reign that they managed to pass through the English parliament an act enforcing an oath of abjuration of the pretender.[1]

Even before this it had been proposed to enforce such an oath in Ireland. A bill for this purpose was suggested in the Irish privy council in 1692, but was not proceeded with.[2] When the plan was revived in 1697 it met with little approval. King, then bishop of Derry, opposed it and defended his action vigorously,[3] and the most influential of the other bishops took the same course.[4] In August, while the bill was still under consideration, Robert Harley wrote to Sir Edward Harley of the ill results that would follow its passing: 'We are pulling everything down about the house as fast as we can'.[5] Though the matter was dropped for the moment the possibility of its revival remained.[6] But in the end it was an act of the English parliament which applied the oath to Ireland.[7] The special interest of the Irish abjuration oath has its origin in this fact. For with its usual ignorance of Irish affairs the English parliament failed to adapt the act of King William's reign to suit conditions in Ireland, with the result that the oath was to be imposed on

[1] 13 & 14 Wm III, c. 6.

[2] *Cal. S. P. dom., Wm III (addenda)*, p. 223.

[3] Bp King to Abp Tenison of Canterbury, 30 Nov. 1697 (King corr. T.C.D., N. 3. 1. pp. 136–7; printed in Mant, *Ch. of Ire.*, p. 78, with date wrongly given as 30 Oct. 1697).

[4] Phillips, *Ch. of Ire.*, iii. 165.

[5] *Portland MSS*, iii. 587.

[6] Alexander McCracken to Joshua Dawson, no date, c. 1702 (Crosslé papers, P.R.O.N.I., T.780, p. 59).

[7] 1 Anne 2 c. 17 (1703). This merely extended 13 Wm III c. 6 to Ireland. For terms of the oath see Grant Robertson, *Select statutes* (5th ed., London, 1928), pp. 160–1.

all 'preachers and teachers of separate congregations'. Now though since the time of Charles II a royal pension had been paid to the protestant dissenting ministers of Ulster, neither the common nor the statute law of Ireland recognised the existence of 'separate congregations'. In spite of this it was clear that the act could be made to apply to these protestant dissenters and that they must obey it. Even so the historian might have found little to interest him in the business had not some three or four presbyterian ministers managed to read into the words of the oath a meaning which was probably as far from the intentions of those who framed it as it was from the minds of the most of those who took it.[1]

Those protestant dissenters who objected to the oath based their main opposition on the ground that the wording of it obliged them to recognise and defend the existing establishment in church as well as in state. This, they said, not only meant giving their full approval to the laws which deprived them of their religious liberty, but, strictly interpreted, would imply acceptance of the whole episcopal system. A further point made against the oath was that it asserted as a fact what was at best a conjecture, namely that the pretender was not the son of James II.[2] The leader of these 'non-jurors' was John McBride, the chief presbyterian minister in Belfast, who had already aroused the hostility of the ecclesiastical authorities.[3] At his instance the annual presbyterian synod for 1703 was called a month earlier than had been originally arranged, to discuss the matter.[4] This synod does not seem to have reached any definite conclusion. But it is clear that McBride and some others failed to take the oath. This appears from a proposal brought forward by the committee of accounts of the Irish commons that since McBride and McCracken had failed to qualify they should be deprived of their share of *regium donum*.[5] There is no evidence that this proposal was carried out at this time.

After this initial threat to enforce the oath the matter seems to have been allowed to drop. In the same year McCracken wrote to his friend

---

[1] The conformists in general seem to have taken the oath without hesitation.

[2] 'The reasons of the non-jurors in Ireland', in *Wodrow correspondence*, i. 158–62.

[3] His 'synod sermon' of 1698 had caused a great uproar. He was called to Dublin, presumably before the privy council, but dismissed with a warning (—to Wodrow, 17 Oct. 1698, P.R.O.N.I., T.525). As late as 1719 the sermon is mentioned by Abp King as an example of presbyterian arrogance (King to Abp Wake of Canterbury, 2 June 1719, Mant, *Ch. of Ire.*, p. 333).

[4] *Rec. gen. syn.*, i. 71.

[5] *Commons' jn. Ire.*, iii. 50.

in Dublin castle, Joshua Dawson, concerning the oath : 'I have not heard of any justice that hath or is concerning themselves about it only some proctor or such officers of the bishop's court'.[1] Wodrow, writing several years later, says, 'It was about the seventeen four or five when that oath was violently pressed in Ireland, and Mr. John McBride and Mr. Alexander McCracken were obliged to leave their charges for refusing it'.[2] But though in 1704 the judges at Carrickfergus ordered the grand jury of Antrim to present the non-jurors, nothing was done.[3] Later in the same year the sheriff of Antrim offered £500 for an information against McCracken.[4] This also failed, for in January 1705 he was still at Lisburn[5] and was present at the synod of that year. He was present again in 1706, but by this time McBride was in exile.[6]

At the synod of 1706 McCracken and two other non-jurors, Gideon Jacque and Thomas Stirling, gave assurance of their loyalty to the queen and attachment to the protestant interest.[7] The two latter do not seem to have been troubled, nor was McCracken till some years later. For this respite he regarded himself as indebted to the government. But early in 1710 proceedings against him on account of the oath were once more threatened.[8] Wodrow attributes this renewed attack to the tory reaction and the Sacheverellite agitation.[9] McCracken himself, in his report of the matter to Dawson, makes out that the prosecution is simply the work of three justices of the peace, and enquires how far the government will help him in returning to Ireland to settle his affairs.[10] For this time the threat had been carried out and by September 1710 McCracken had fled to Scotland. But the double fact, first that McCracken was the only

[1] Crosslé papers, P.R.O.N.I., T.780, p. 72. It is clear from the correspondence between them that McCracken and Dawson were on intimate terms and the former seems to have counted on getting early information of any new move by government from his friend.

[2] Wodrow to James Hog, 30 Nov. 1710 (*Wodrow correspondence*, i. 191).

[3] McCracken to Dawson, 22 Apr. 1704 (Crosslé papers, P.R.O.N.I., T. 780, p. 72).

[4] Same to same, 5 May 1704 (ibid., p. 73).

[5] Same to same, Jan. 1704 (ibid., p. 71).

[6] For this and later attendances of McCracken and McBride at synods see appendix to this chapter. For McBride's exile see McCracken to Dawson, 2 Sept. 1706 (Crosslé papers, p. 64).

[7] *Rec. gen. syn.*, i. 121.

[8] McCracken to Dawson, 23 Mar. 1710 (Crosslé papers, P.R.O.N.I., T.780, pp. 61–2).

[9] R. Wodrow to James Hog, 30 Nov. 1710 (*Wodrow correspondence*, i. 192).

[10] McCracken to Dawson, 21 Sept. 1710 (Crosslé papers, P.R.O.N.I., T.780, pp. 60–1).

person seriously troubled at this time and secondly that he was able to leave the country, shows how local and spasmodic was the persecution.

This immunity of protestant dissenting non-jurors was one of the things complained of by the house of lords in their address to the queen in 1711.[1] The principal remedy suggested was the complete withdrawal of *regium donum*. The government did not immediately follow out this suggestion, but it seems likely that in the following year payment to McCracken, McBride and another non-juring minister, Riddle, was suspended.[2] Riddle was a man of little importance, but the prominence of McBride's position marked him out for attack.

He had left the country in 1706 and remained in Scotland for some years. He was back in Ireland by 1709 and suffered some little inconvenience in 1710 when McCracken was forced into exile.[3] But after the outburst in the parliament of 1711 he seems to have felt himself threatened, and in 1712 went back to Scotland. By the following spring, however, he was thinking of returning,[4] and he was present at the synod of 1713. The synod of the previous year, at which neither he nor McCracken had been present, had strongly urged all those who had entered the ministry since the abjuration oath was imposed and who had not taken it to do so as quickly as possible.[5] The presbyterians had plenty of other grievances and did not want to give their enemies any additional weapon against them. Those who refused the oath would have the sympathy of their colleagues in any consequent sufferings but could hardly expect their cause to be made the cause of all.

McCracken's chief hope now seems to have rested in the English government and he went to London to forward his cause there.[6] But action depended largely upon the attitude of the lord lieutenant;[7] and Ormond, whose government was drawing to a close, was apparently unwilling to meddle in the affair.[8] Towards the end of 1712 the English lord treasurer (Oxford) had made some indirect enquiries from the

[1] *Lords' jn. Ire.*, ii. 410–11. See p. 54, above.

[2] McCracken to McBride, no date, *c.* 1712 (Crosslé papers, P.R.O.N.I., T.780, pp. 58–9). There is a list of presbyterian ministers to whom *regium donum* was to be paid for Christmas quarter 1712; from this list McBride, McCracken and Riddle are excluded (ibid., pp. 40–1, King's letters in Auditor-general's office, vol. ix).

[3] Wodrow to James Hog, 30 Nov. 1710 (*Wodrow correspondence*, i. 192).

[4] Same to John McBride, 12 Mar. 1713 (ibid., i. 426).

[5] *Rec. gen. syn.*, i. 283.

[6] McCracken to Dawson, 5 Mar. 1712 (Crosslé papers, P.R.O.N.I., T.780, p. 60).

[7] Southwell to Dawson, 22 Aug. 1713 (ibid., p. 51).

[8] William Wogan to Dawson, 5 Sept. 1713 (ibid., p. 51).

Irish chancellor, Sir Constantine Phipps, about the effect of suspending proceedings against the non-juring dissenters. The chancellor suggested that such a suspension would place the Irish dissenters in a more favourable position than the English dissenters.[1] Beyond these enquiries the English government seems to have done nothing. So when McBride and McCracken returned in 1713 they had no guarantee of protection against their enemies, and the influence of their friends in London and Dublin was not sufficient to restrain the activities of the local magistrates.[2] This could only be done by special directions from the English government, and though both McBride and McCracken were reported to have claimed assurances of protection from the lord treasurer and even from the queen, such assurances had not in fact been given. At the same time, it is clear that the government did not order their prosecution, which was entirely the work of local justices.[3] The two most active of these were Westenra Waring, high sheriff of Down, and Captain Brent Spencer of Lisburn. Between them they had McBride in hiding and McCracken imprisoned in Carrickfergus before the end of 1713.[4]

The attitude of the English government to the fate of these non-jurors makes it clear that the anti-presbyterian agitation in Ireland during the later part of Queen Anne's reign was not merely the reflection of the tory reaction in England. This is borne out by the fact that the triumph of the whigs in August 1714 did not immediately improve the position of the presbyterians in Ireland. Though in May 1715 McBride wrote a jubilant letter to Wodrow, describing the discomfiture of their opponents, 'The whigs in this kingdom carry all before them . . .,' yet McCracken was still in prison.[5] The invasion scare of 1715 naturally produced a desire to conciliate all possible supporters, the attempt to enforce the abjuration oath was dropped, and in 1716 McCracken was released and for the first time since 1710 felt it safe to attend the synod. In the previous year, the presbyterians had made a move to have the oath abolished or modified, and some negotiations to that end took place in London,[6] but no change was made. Perhaps the failure of the rising of 1715 made insistence on the oath seem less necessary, perhaps

[1] Sir Constantine Phipps to lord treasurer, 26 Dec. 1712 (*Portland MSS*, v. 254–5).

[2] McBride gives an account of the treatment received by McCracken and himself in a letter to Wodrow, 4 Aug. 1713 (*Wodrow correspondence*, i. 483).

[3] Joshua Dawson to Southwell, 4 & 8 Aug. 1713 (Crosslé papers, P.R.O.N.I., T.780, pp. 44–5).

[4] Crosslé papers, pp. 70–1; *P.R.I. rep. D.K. 30*, pp. 55–6; R. Wodrow to William Carstairs, 8 Dec. 1713 (*Wodrow correspondence*, i. 529).

[5] McBride to R. Wodrow, 16 May 1715 (ibid., ii. 47).

[6] *H.M.C. rep. 3*, app., p. 374.

the number of those who objected to the wording seemed too small to deserve special consideration, perhaps, as is more likely, the government took the simplest way of getting rid of a troublesome measure by simply allowing it to fall into disuse. The next occasion on which the oath was used as a means of persecution was when one presbyterian sect found it a convenient weapon against another.[1]

The whole episode of the abjuration oath throws important light on the position of the Irish protestant dissenters at the time. It is clear that the government regarded the oath merely as a security against hidden jacobites and did not intend it to be a new burden on the dissenters. But when it appeared that the oath could become a weapon in the hands of their persecutors the government did very little for them. Only after the events of 1 August 1714 had placed the whigs in an almost impregnable position was the government ready and able to interfere effectively in checking the persecuting zeal of its local representatives. The truth was that the government still depended largely upon these local representatives, the justices of the peace, for the execution of its mandates. Control over them was often slow. Interference was sometimes regarded as undesirable. Even Joshua Dawson, friendly to McCracken though he was, thought that any attempt by the government to stop the prosecutions begun by Waring and Spencer against the non-jurors would be dangerous.[2] McCracken, on the other hand affected to regret that the queen's power was insufficient to restrain the magistrates. 'As I am truly for the queen and her government so shall I be sorry to find her power of relieving the peaceable subjects from the persecuting spirit of three justices so eclipsed that they are able to declare that none need apply to her for refuge for she hath no power to relieve them. If this be found so upon trial, we cannot help it, only shall regret our hardships and endeavour to live in or out of gaol, and pray for the queen who is not able to relieve us from men who (it seems) are stronger than she. . . .'[3]

Dawson's point of view represented more accurately the circumstances of the time. Government intervention on behalf of the dissenters was spasmodic and often belated, though usually in the long run effective. But their almost complete immunity from the effects of the penal laws against them depended on the connivance of the local authorities, rather than on the favour of the government, English or Irish. The history of the abjuration oath shows that such connivance was not always to be relied upon.

[1] Reid, *History*, iii. 314–6.

[2] Dawson to Southwell, 4 Aug. 1713 (Crosslé papers, P.R.O.N.I., T.780, p. 44).

[3] McCracken to Dawson, 1 Aug. 1713 (ibid., p. 64).

APPENDIX

ATTENDANCE of John McBride and Alexander McCracken at synods,
1704–16 (from *Records of the general synod of Ulster*)

Year	McBride	McCracken
1704	P	P
1705	P	P
1706	ex	P
1707	ex	P
1708	ex	P
1709	P	P
1710	P	P
1711	P	ex
1712	ex	ex
1713	P	ex
1714	ex	ex
1715	P	ex
1716	P	P

P—present.
ex—excused.

VII

THE TOLERATION ACT OF 1719

The importance of the accession of George I to the Irish presbyterians can best be seen in the depression of their enemies the high churchmen. Both the lords justices and Archbishop King complain of the attitude of those clergy who omitted to pray for the new royal family and made an indirect attack on the king by preaching against the Lutheran doctrine of consubstantiation.[1] No doubt the bitterness shown by a section of the clergy was due to fears that the new government would prove less devoted to the maintenance of the church's privileges than the old, fears which were in some measure justified by the failure to call a convocation. The way seemed prepared for a general reversal of the existing situation, involving not only the legal toleration of protestant dissenters, but their admission to public employment by the repeal of the sacramental test. The presbyterians themselves expected no less, and up to a point their expectations were answered. *Regium donum* was resumed and increased; McCracken was released from prison; the attempt to enforce the abjuration oath ended.[2] But here the process stopped. Although the persecution, local and spasmodic at worst, had ended, the presbyterians were legally no better off than they had been. Only after five years were they granted a legal toleration; and even then the sacramental test remained.

This delay was not the fault of the English government, which from the first showed itself favourable to the presbyterians. It was due to the power which the Irish church still possessed of resisting any policy of which it disapproved. For though the church had been weakened by the change of government in 1714 its influence was not destroyed; and in its first trial of strength with the new ministry it came off best. The dispute arose over the position of presbyterian officers in the militia and army. In 1715 alarm was caused by the possibility of an invasion by the

[1] Lords justices to Stanhope, 22 Jan. 1716 (T.S.P.I., T.448, p. 208). Abp King to Bp Ashe of Clogher, 19 Aug. 1714; same to Bp Stearne of Dromore, 26 Aug. 1714 (Mant, *Ch. of Ire.*, p. 275); same to Dean Mossom, 10 Sept. 1715; same to Dr Jenkins, 14 Apr. 1716 (King corr. T.C.D., transcript).

[2] For *regium donum* see later in this chapter and ch. X below. For McCracken and the abjuration oath see ch. VI above.

pretender, accompanied by a rising of the Roman catholics.[1] To meet
the danger the militia was called out, and after some hesitation presbyterian gentlemen to whom commissions had been offered decided to
accept them.[2] By doing so they laid themselves open to the penalties
provided by the sacramental test. Naturally no action was taken against
them; though Archbishop King professed alarm lest papists might slip
in under cover of being dissenters.[3]

Though safe for the time being, those presbyterians who had accepted
commissions wished to secure their future position by getting parliament
to pass an act of indemnity. This was thought a convenient occasion to
press for something more. The commons suggested that the sacramental
test should be suspended in so far as it affected the militia for ever and
in so far as it affected the army for ten years.[4] According to Archbishop
King this was pushed through under actual fear of invasion, and the
circumstances make this likely enough.[5] The proposal was included in
the heads of a bill for the security of the king's person, to be submitted
to England. In the house of lords the bishops brought in heads of a
similar bill omitting all reference to the test.[6] The Irish privy council, in
considering these heads, tried to form a single bill out of them. The
debate centred round the proposal to admit dissenters to commissions
in the army. As a compromise it was suggested that they should be
admitted, not for ten years, but for the duration of the rebellion or of
the current session of parliament. The bishops and their supporters in
the council at first agreed but later changed their minds. In spite of this
the compromise bill was carried by one vote and sent to England.[7] The
lords justices (Grafton and Galway) were in a dilemma. On the one
hand, they did not wish to alienate the dissenters; on the other, the bill
as it stood was almost certain to be lost in the house of lords owing to
the opposition of the bishops. They seem to have thought, however, that
it would be unwise to have the test clause omitted in England as that
would be a great discouragement to the presbyterians.[8] Archbishop

[1] Abp King to Robert Howard, 30 July 1715; to Bp Nicolson of Carlisle,
30 July 1715; to Bp Ashe of Clogher, 6 Aug. 1715 (King corr. T.C.D.,
transcript). Lords justices to ——, 14 Nov. 1715 (T.S.P.I., T.448, p. 151).

[2] Crosslé papers, P.R.O.N.I., T.780, pp. 54–5.

[3] Abp King to Thomas Knox, 18 Aug. 1715 (King corr. T.C.D., transcript).

[4] Charles Delafaye to ——, 30 Jan. 1716 (T.S.P.I., T. 448, p. 213).

[5] Abp King to Abp Wake of Canterbury, 24 Mar. 1716 (King corr. T.C.D.,
transcript).

[6] *Lords' jn. Ire.*, ii. 504; T.S.P.I., T.448, pp. 229, 238.

[7] Lords justices to Stanhope, 16 Mar. 1716 (T.S.P.I., T.448, p. 256).

[8] Lords justices to Stanhope, 28 Mar. & 22 May 1716 (T.S.P.I., T.448,
pp. 273, 301).

King, on the other hand, did his best to have the clause remodelled by the English government and used his influence with the archbishop of Canterbury to this end.[1] King's task was made more difficult by the fact that the English government not only wished to oblige the dissenters but also believed that the proposal for suspending the test was strongly supported by the Irish gentry.[2] In the end the bill came back to Ireland, though in what form cannot be ascertained; but all the circumstances indicate that the clause in favour of the protestant dissenters was retained. After some discussion in the house of commons the bill was dropped and two resolutions were passed instead:

'That such of his majesty's protestant dissenting subjects of this kingdom as have taken commissions in the militia, or acted in the commission of array, have hereby done a seasonable service to his majesty's royal person and government, and the protestant interest in this kingdom'.

'That any person who shall commence a prosecution against any dissenter who has accepted, or shall accept, of a commission in the array or militia, is an enemy to King George and the protestant interest, and a friend to the pretender'.[3]

Reid's view is that the bill was abandoned by the lords justices in deference to the wishes of the bishops, and that the resolutions express the disappointment and determination of the commons.[4] But this requires some modification. First, the bill was postponed in committee of the whole house—this was equal to rejection by the commons themselves.[5] Secondly, and apart from this, it is by no means clear that the commons were whole-heartedly sympathetic to the protestant dissenters, of whom there were only about half-a-dozen in the house.[6] The heads of the bill had been passed, at least according to the churchmen, under pressure of events; and the immediate danger had now disappeared.[7] Of the two resolutions which replaced the bill the first, passed unanimously, had never been opposed by King and his friends, and the

[1] Abp King to Abp Wake of Canterbury, 26 Mar. & 26 Apr. 1716; same to Dr Jenkins, 14 Apr. 1716 (King corr. T.C.D., transcript).

[2] Robert Howard to Abp King, London, 17 Mar. 1716; same to same, 12 Apr. 1716 (*H.M.C. rep. 2*, app. pp. 251–2). The importance attached to the bill can be seen from a reference to it in the *Stuart papers*, ii. 84.

[3] *Commons' jn. Ire.*, iv. 255 (5 June 1716).

[4] Reid, *History*, iii. 79. This view is also supported by Froude, *Ire.*, i. 430.

[5] Abp King to Abp Wake of Canterbury, 5 June 1716 (King corr. T.C.D.).

[6] Same to Bp Ashe of Clogher, 8 Feb. 1716 (ibid., transcript).

[7] Howard to Abp King, 17 Mar. 1716 (*H.M.C. rep.*, 2 app., p. 251); Abp King to Abp Wake of Canterbury, 24 Mar. 1716 (King corr. T.C.D., transcript).

second was passed only after discussion. These circumstances make it more likely that the settlement of June 1716 was a compromise, either between two parties in the commons or between the commons and the government, than that it was an arbitrary decision of the lords justices acting under episcopal pressure.

Though the church interest had thus won the first round in the contest over toleration and the repeal of the test neither the presbyterians nor the government gave up the struggle. The sympathy of the government counteracted much of the petty persecution to which the presbyterians were still subjected in some districts. For example, the lords justices interfered to try to make universal the practice whereby presbyterians chosen as churchwardens could act through substitutes.[1] Though the marriage question still continued to give trouble,[2] King's opinion in 1718 was that the protestant dissenters of Ireland enjoyed as much liberty as those of England.[3] This, however, even if true did not satisfy the presbyterians. In 1716 they decided to send commissioners to England when occasion should present itself; in the meantime presbyterian officers should continue to act in the militia.[4] In the following year their chance seemed to come with the proposal to repeal the English occasional conformity act, for by this time they were convinced that if the test was to be repealed it must be by act of the English parliament. King was so convinced of the danger that he wrote to his friends urging them to use their influence against any interference in England with Irish ecclesiastical affairs.[5] This was while King was at Bath. On his return to Ireland he seems to have been satisfied that the government had no idea of meddling with the test;[6] and in fact nothing was done at this time. Early in 1718 there were fresh rumours of an attempt at repeal, but these also came to nothing.[7]

This temporary shelving of the question was partly due to the presby-

[1] The practice dates at least from the late 17th century. Bp King to Foley, 9 May 1693 (King corr. T.C.D.). In 1716 a dispute on the question arose in the parish of Antrim and the lords justices urged moderation on the bishop and rector (Marsh's Lib., MS. Z. 3. 1. 1. xiii).

[2] Gilbert Kennedy to R. Wodrow, 1716, quoted in J. Stevenson, *Two centuries of life in Down*, p. 163.

[3] Abp King to Bp Smith of Down, 5 July 1718 (King corr. T.C.D., transcript).

[4] *Rec. gen. syn.*, i. 409–10.

[5] Abp King to Marmaduke Coghill, 6 May 1717; same to Samuel Molyneux, 6 May 1717; same to Abp Wake of Canterbury, 5 June 1717 (King corr. T.C.D., transcript).

[6] Same to same, 28 Aug. 1717 (ibid.).

[7] Same to L. C. J. Whitsel, 6 Jan. 1718 (ibid.).

terians themselves. In June 1716, just after the failure of the toleration bill, they agreed with the protestant dissenters of Dublin to send a joint commission to England to press for another bill 'at such a junction as should afterwards be agreed on'.[1] Two years later the commissioners had not yet set out.[2] A considerable part of the intervening time was taken up in discussions about the terms on which toleration should be demanded or accepted. Since the government was not likely to extend toleration to a body whose principles were not clearly laid down the presbyterians had to decide whether they should present the Westminster confession as the only statement of their belief, or be willing, should the government reject that, to abide by some other formula, or even by a modified form of the thirty-nine articles. Those who refused to budge from the Westminster confession were inclined to regard the others as latitudinarians, seizing this opportunity to bring in the principles of Hoadley.[3] While discussion went on action was delayed.

But the anomalous position of the Irish protestant dissenters was not forgotten; and about this time another circumstance helped to bring it to the attention of those in power. This was the flow of Ulster protestants to north America, which King mentions as beginning in 1717.[4] Though King maintained that the emigrants were not all dissenters but included churchmen, and that the cause of emigration was not persecution but high rents, the presbyterians insisted that they were being driven out by the hardships which they had to suffer, and dwelt on the consequent weakening of the English interest in the north of Ireland.[5] Though it was not until ten years later that the government became really alarmed about the growth of emigration, we may reasonably suppose that the beginning of it had something to do with preparing the way for the toleration bill of 1719. Apart from this it is hard to find any special reason for the revival of the toleration project at this time, though the government may have been influenced by the renewed danger of a jacobite rising backed by Spain and Sweden. The joint commission to represent protestant dissenters of north and south had not yet been chosen.[6] Some negotiations were going on in London, but they seem to

---

[1] *Rec. gen. syn.*, i. 410. [2] Ibid., i. 478.

[3] R. Wodrow to Robert Black, — Sept. 1716; A. McCracken to R. Wodrow, 1 Feb. 1717; William Wright to same, — 1718 (*Wodrow correspondence*, ii. 212, 238, 389 note). See also *Rec. gen. syn.*, i. 395–6.

[4] Abp King to Abp Wake of Canterbury, 6 Feb. 1718, in C. S. King, *A great archbishop of Dublin*, p. 207.

[5] Cotton Mather to R. Wodrow, 6 Aug. 1718; R. Wodrow to Cotton Mather, 29 Jan. 1719 (*Wodrow correspondence*, ii. 424, 426).

[6] *Rec. gen. syn.*, i. 478.

have been concerned mainly if not wholly with a prospective increase in *regium donum*.[1] The general synod of 1718, finding that Colonel Upton intended to go to Bristol, arranged with him to get into touch with their friends in London and report on the possibilities of something being done 'in what concerns this church';[2] but the whole transaction appears to be vague and casual. There is nothing in all this to indicate that the presbyterians were pushing their claim for toleration with any vigour. On the whole it would seem that it was the English ministry which pressed on the business. In February 1719 a sort of ministerial conference was held in London at which were present, among others, the duke of Bolton, who was shortly to go to Ireland as lord lieutenant, Lord Stanhope and Lord Sunderland. Here the whole subject of relief for the Irish protestant dissenters was discussed. It was apparently *after* this that Colonel Upton entered into negotiations with the English ministry.[3] If this is so, then the whole initiative in the passing of the toleration bill was on the side of the government.

This conclusion, though likely enough to be accurate, must be accepted with caution; for contemporary accounts enable us to trace the history of the bill from two viewpoints only—that of the Irish government, and that of the church opposition, notably Archbishop King. From these accounts we get a picture of negotiations between the bishops, the house of commons, the lord lieutenant, and the English ministry. But it is hard to see what part the dissenters themselves played in the matter. In the early stages they were probably mere spectators. Their influence in the house of commons was negligible, and it was there that everything of importance was done. The bill sent over from England was dropped, the 'heads of a bill' brought in by the chancellor of the exchequer and sponsored by the Irish government were dropped,[4] and their place was taken by a set of heads originating solely in the Irish house of commons. A time-table of these events is instructive. Parliament met on June 6. No attempt was made to bring in the bill which had been drawn up in England; but on July 4 permission was given to bring in heads of a bill to ease the dissenters. This was meant to be a government measure and the committee in charge included the chancellor of the exchequer and the solicitor-general. On July 6 permission was given

---

[1] Ibid., 480. [2] Ibid., 478.

[3] Bolton to ——, 27 June 1719 (T.S.P.I., T.519, pp. 146 ff.). It is not unreasonable to see some connection between the repeal of the English schism and occasional conformity acts in 1719 (5 Geo. I c. 4) and the government's desire to resume its efforts on behalf of the protestant dissenters in Ireland. But there is no indication of the nature of the connection.

[4] Bolton to Craggs, 7 July, 16 July 1719 (T.S.P.I., T.519, pp. 158–9, 171–2).

to a different committee to bring in heads of a similar bill. These heads were presented the next day and after some revision were ready for transmission to England on July 16.[1] In all this two things are specially significant, the speed with which the second committee got to work, and the fact that nothing more is heard of the first set of heads. This lends weight to other evidence that the house of commons took the matter into its own hands and that the government was glad to get a toleration bill of any sort without trying very hard to dictate the form of it.

Once the Irish government had abandoned the attempt to control the framing of the heads of the toleration bill, any chance that the presbyterians ever had of influencing its terms disappeared. But when the draft bill was sent over to England it was open to them to try to have some alterations made there. Against this, it must be remembered that the Irish commons had accepted the principle of toleration without enthusiasm and were not likely to make any further concessions. The probable result of an attempt to alter the bill in favour of the dissenters was foreshadowed in the debate in the Irish council before the draft was sent to England. There Archbishop King and his friends laboured hard to restrict the terms of the proposed toleration, and so evenly was the council divided that only the lord lieutenant's casting vote prevented their success.[2] In the end one clause was added in England in favour of persons who should qualify themselves under the terms of the act after prosecutions had actually been begun against them. The wording of this aroused some fears in the house of commons, but the lawyers were able to offer a satisfactory explanation and the bill passed by a majority of eight to one.[3] In the house of lords the struggle was more serious. At last the measure was carried by a narrow majority; there were present thirteen spiritual and nineteen temporal lords; nine of the former and seven of the latter registered their dissent in the journals of the house.[4]

The alarm which the dissentients express hardly seems justified by the terms of the act. The penalties for non-attendance at the parish church, laid down by the Elizabethan act of uniformity, were not to be enforced against protestant dissenters who should qualify for exemption by taking an oath of allegiance, an oath of abjuration of the papal power to depose sovereigns, an oath of abjuration of the pretender, and by signing a declaration against transubstantiation and other distinctively Roman catholic doctrines. Protestant dissenting ministers were, on the

[1] *Commons' jn. Ire.*, ii. 490, 501, 503, 505, 516, 517.

[2] Abp King to Abp Wake of Canterbury, 1 Aug. 1719 (Mant, *Ch. of Ire.*, pp. 334 ff.).

[3] Webster to Delafaye, 15 Oct. 1719 (T.S.P.I., T.519, p. 219).

[4] *Lords' jn. Ire.*, ii. 663.

same terms, freed from the penalties imposed by the act of uniformity of 1665 upon all ministers who, without being episcopally ordained, should celebrate the sacrament of the Lord's supper. No person who had qualified under these terms could be prosecuted for mere non-conformity; if he qualified after such prosecution had begun proceedings must at once stop. But the jurisdiction of ecclesiastical courts, except for mere non-conformity, was expressly maintained. There was to be no exemption from tithes or other parochial dues. Protestant dissenting ministers were relieved from acting as churchwardens, constables etc., but other protestant dissenters must, when chosen, perform the duty, either in person or by a deputy acceptable to the bishop. All dissenting places of worship must be registered and no meetings might be held behind locked or bolted doors. A special form of affirmation was provided for quakers; but persons denying the doctrine of the Holy Trinity as set forth in the thirty-nine articles were expressly excluded from the benefits of the act.[1]

During this struggle the presbyterians seem to have made no official move in support of the bill; though the exchange of pamphlets, never wholly dropped, was for a time intensified. This inactivity was partly due to the fact that the struggle was decided in parliament, where presbyterian influence was slight. But it probably arose as much from lack of interest as from lack of opportunity. The bill did not contain what the presbyterians really wanted—repeal of the sacramental test.[2] Without this, the toleration gave them no more than they already possessed.[3] It legalised but did not extend the existing indulgence.

In tracing the history of this toleration bill it is hard to escape the impression that the position of the protestant dissenters was a matter of little interest to most of those involved. The English ministry regarded the measure as one which they were bound in principle and policy to forward as well as they could, rather because some such move was expected of a whig government than out of any sympathy with Irish presbyterians; and many of those who supported it in Ireland supported it on no other ground than that it was recommended from England. The commons, King says, had no great liking for the bill, 'but being so hardly pressed in the lord lieutenant's speech, they seemed under a necessity to do something, which might be reckoned a compliance'.[4] On

[1] 6 Geo. I c. 5 (Ireland).

[2] Bolton to ——, 27 June 1719 (T.S.P.I., T.519, pp. 146 ff.).

[3] Abp King to Abp Wake of Canterbury, 2 June 1719 (Mant, *Ch. of Ire.*, p. 333 ff).

[4] Abp King to Abp Wake of Canterbury, 1 Aug. 1719 (Mant, *Ch. of Ire.*, pp. 334 ff.). For lord lieutenant's speech see *Lords' jn. Ire.*, ii. 604; lords' reply, ibid., 604, 605, 606; commons' reply, *Commons' jn. Ire.*, iv. 499.

the other side there was no open opposition to the principle of toleration, but only to such toleration as might weaken the position of the
established church. But since in previous parliaments the question of
toleration had generally aroused a stormy struggle between Irish high
churchmen and English whigs, so now to oppose or to limit the legal
toleration suggested by the English government seemed the most obvious
way of displaying loyalty to the church. Archbishop King was generally
given the credit, even by his opponents, of being honest if obstinate in
his opinions, but his fears about the results of the toleration act seem
far-fetched and unreal. He wrote to the archbishop of Canterbury:
'I fear we shall all feel the effects of it; and, in truth, I can't see how our
church can stand here, if God do not, by a peculiar and unforseen
providence, support it'.[1] Such fears have little connection with the facts;
the act did no more than give legal recognition to the position which the
Irish protestant dissenters had occupied since 1714. For the high churchmen it was the symbol rather than the substance of defeat. Their energy
in opposing and limiting the proposed toleration arose largely from the
suspicion that the government intended to go far beyond the suggestions
put forward in the lord lieutenant's speech at the opening of parliament.
This suspicion was well founded. The English government's original
idea had been an entire repeal of the sacramental test, and Bolton had
some difficulty in persuading them that such a measure was impracticable.[2] All this serves to show that the opposition to toleration was
merely tactical, intended not to defeat it but to limit its scope. As we
have seen, the commons secured the abandonment of the government
measure by substituting one of their own. A similar move was attempted
in the house of lords, but it was made too late and failed.[3]

The indifference of the presbyterians to the passage of the bill has
already been explained; and it was probably accompanied by the fear
that the establishment of legal toleration would weaken the case for
removal of the test. But this indifference was known[4] and only makes it
more difficult to understand why the English ministry made such a push
for a measure which would inevitably arouse opposition among church-

[1] Abp King to Abp Wake of Canterbury, 10 Nov. 1719 (Mant, *Ch. of Ire.*,
p. 337).

[2] Bolton to ——, 27 June 1719 (T.S.P.I., T.519, pp. 146 ff.).

[3] The lords' draft bill was presented to the lord lieutenant for transmission
to England on Sept. 28. On Oct. 3 the commons' bill, having returned from
England, had its first reading in the lower house, and on Oct. 6 in the upper
house (*Lords' jn. Ire.*, ii. 641, 653; *Commons' jn. Ire.*, iv. 642).

[4] Abp King to Abp Wake of Canterbury, 2 June 1719 (Mant, *Ch. of Ire.*,
pp. 333 ff.).

men, without establishing any claim on the gratitude of protestant dissenters. Their experience over the militia question in 1716 should have enabled them to gauge the strength of the opposition to toleration in the Irish parliament. Yet their actions indicate no such knowledge. They first announced their intention of granting substantial relief to the presbyterians. Next they sent over a bill for that purpose. But on the first show of determined opposition they allowed their bill to drop and accepted an almost worthless substitute. One explanation, though a partial one, of this difficulty may be found in the theory that the house of commons had really been strongly in favour of the measures proposed for the relief of the protestant dissenters in 1716, and that the English ministry counted on this support when they sent over the bill which had to be so speedily abandoned in 1719. But this explanation, improbable in itself, only serves to accentuate another difficulty. It has already been pointed out that the commons were probably by no means enthusiastic in favour of the indemnity bill of 1716. It is, at any rate, absolutely certain that between 1716 and 1719 the feeling in the house of commons against the protestant dissenters had become stronger. This in itself is a difficult problem. It becomes much more difficult if the change is represented as one from enthusiastic support to uncompromising opposition. In the absence of definite evidence any theory must be based on an economy of hypothesis; and the most rational explanation seems to be that the English government having learned nothing by the disputes of 1716 sent over a bill which was intended to satisfy the claims of the presbyterians; the opposition to this so surprised them and threatened to make things so difficult for the lord lieutenant that they were glad to accept any bill at all.

If the conduct of the English ministry requires explanation so does the conduct of the Irish parliament, especially that of the house of lords. For in this year there was passed, with little opposition, another measure, which marks the first really successful attack on the sacramental test. This was an indemnity act,[1] by which office-holders who had failed to take the test according to 2 Anne c. 6 were given until 25 March 1720 to do so. The opponents of toleration do not seem to have realised that a privilege of this sort is more easily granted than revoked, and this indemnity act proved to be the first of a long series.[2]

These two acts of 1719 settled the position of the Irish protestant dissenters for over half a century. They enjoyed a legal toleration, subject to minor annoyances on such matters as marriages and church-

[1] 6 Geo. I c. 9 (Ireland).
[2] See appendix to this chapter.

wardenships. The sacramental test, though still on the statute-book, was modified by indemnity acts and, increasingly, by custom. Even so it remained the chief grievance of the presbyterians and for over fifteen years their political activities were largely directed towards its removal.

APPENDIX

(INDEMNITY ACTS from *The statutes at large, passed in the parliaments held in Ireland*, Dublin, 1786)

1719	6 Geo. I	c. 9	An act indemnifying those who had failed to take the oaths etc. and the sacrament according to 2 Anne c. 6. They are to qualify by	25 Mar. 1720
1725	12 Geo. I	c. 6	Time extended to	1 Aug. 1726
1729	3 Geo. II	c. 6		1 Aug. 1730
1731	5 Geo. II	c. 5		1 Aug. 1732
1733	7 Geo. II	c. 4		1 Aug. 1734
1737	11 Geo. II	c. 10		1 Aug. 1738
1739	13 Geo. II	c. 7		1 Aug. 1740
1741	15 Geo. II	c. 4		1 Aug. 1742
1743	17 Geo. II	c. 9		1 Aug. 1744
1747	21 Geo. II	c. 5		25 Mar. 1749
1749	23 Geo. II	c. 7		25 Mar. 1751
1751	25 Geo. II	c. 7		25 Mar. 1753
1755	29 Geo. II	c. 2		25 Mar. 1756
1757	30 Geo. II	c. 4		1 May 1758
1759	31 Geo. II	c. 3		1 Aug. 1760
1761	1 Geo. III	c. 4		1 Aug. 1762
1763	3 Geo. III	c. 3		1 Aug. 1764
1765	5 Geo. III	c. 11		1 Aug. 1766
1767	7 Geo. III	c. 16		1 Aug. 1768
1771	11 Geo. III	c. 3		1 Aug. 1774
1772	11 & 12 Geo. III	c. 29		1 Aug. 1774 [sic]
1774	13 & 14 Geo. III	c. 13		1 Aug. 1775
1776	15 & 16 Geo. III	c. 5		1 Aug. 1776
1778	17 & 18 Geo. III	c. 5		1 May 1778

THE TOLERATION ACT OF 1719

NOTES

(*a*) From the first renewal (12 Geo. I c. 6) it was stated that no one was to be restored to any office vacated by enforcement of 2 Anne c. 6 (sacramental test; see p. 46 above).

(*b*) In 23 Geo. II c. 7 is a clause stating that no officer who has qualified in England need qualify again in Ireland. This is repeated in the subsequent acts except 1 Geo. III c. 4.

(*c*) The act 7 Geo. III c. 16 contains a clause to the effect that justices of the peace are not to be required to qualify more than once.

(*d*) Even after the repeal of the sacramental test (19 & 20 Geo. III c. 6), indemnity acts were passed: 19 & 20 Geo. III c. 28, extending the time for qualification to 24 June 1781, and 21 & 22 Geo. III c. 7, extending the time to 1 August 1782.

VIII

THE ATTEMPTS TO REPEAL THE
SACRAMENTAL TEST, 1731-3,
AND THEIR FAILURE

It has already been noted that in the period before the toleration act of 1719 the Ulster presbyterians were divided on the question of a statement of their faith, if one should be required by the government, and that those who stood for the Westminster confession, complete and without alternative, looked with some suspicion upon their opponents.[1] Superficially this was no more than a difference on a matter of policy. In reality it went much deeper, for some at least of those who were willing to abandon the Westminster confession wished to do away with subscription to any fixed statement of belief. Almost at the very time of the passage of the toleration act and the first indemnity act, this divergence of opinion, the original occasion of which had now disappeared, produced in the synod of Ulster two opposed parties— 'subscribers' and 'non-subscribers'. It was not until 1726 that the dispute reached some sort of settlement, with the exclusion of the non-subscribers from the synod, and during this interval the presbyterians had little time or energy for political activity.[2] They had been bitterly disappointed that the legislation of 1719 had left the sacramental test intact; even the indemnity act of that year, which expired in 1720, was not renewed until 1725.[3] But the circumstances of the failure had made it clear that no immediate renewal of the attack was likely to be more successful; so it is not surprising that for the next ten years the Ulster presbyterians remained on the whole passive, more concerned with their internal disputes than with political influence or legal status.

But even during this period, attempts were made to secure redress of various minor grievances. So far, no legal indemnity had been given to those protestant dissenters who had accepted commissions in the

[1] See ch. VII, p. 75 above.

[2] *Narrative of the proceedings of the seven general synods of the northern presbyterians in Ireland, with relation to their differences, 1720-26.* By the ministers of the presbytery of Antrim, 1727. This pamphlet of 392 closely printed pages illustrates the extent to which internal controversy had absorbed the attention of the synod.

[3] See appendix to chap. VII, above.

militia without taking the test during the jacobite scare of 1715. It seems that some approach was made to the duke of Bolton early in 1720, probably unofficially, for there is no mention of it in the *Records of the general synod of Ulster*. The duke suggested a parliamentary indemnity, but thought that a royal pardon might be sufficient.[1] Apparently the latter alternative was accepted for no act was passed at that time. The fact that the question, having been postponed in 1716, was raised again in 1720 makes it seem probable that presbyterian officers had retained their commissions, for the Irish house of commons had already made it clear that it approved of the conduct of those who had acted during the period when invasion seemed imminent. Even among high churchmen opposition had been directed only against the proposal that these presbyterian officers should retain their commissions, and that others should be admitted in future.[2] It seems then almost certain that what the presbyterians wanted was not indemnity for having acted as militia officers during the rebellion, but for having retained their commissions when it was over, or for having accepted commissions since that date. It would seem also that the failure to secure a parliamentary indemnity in 1720 did not deter them from continuing to accept commissions, for when at last in 1755 an act was passed throwing the militia open to protestant dissenters it was thought necessary to make it retrospective.[3]

An equally abortive attempt was made to settle another long-standing grievance of the presbyterians—marriages. In 1722 it was resolved to draw up a representation on the subject.[4] Presumably as a result of this a bill to protect protestant dissenters from prosecution on account of marriages performed by their own ministers was prepared, but, in spite of an attempt to tack it to another bill, and after a complicated process of alteration, it was lost in the commons in February 1724.[5]

It is worth while contrasting this failure of the presbyterians with the success of the quakers in securing a relief act which allowed them to make affirmations instead of taking oaths, a privilege which they already enjoyed in certain circumstances, as for example in complying with the terms of the toleration act of 1719.[6] Slight though this concession might be, it was gained by a sect almost entirely without political importance,

[1] Bolton to Craggs, 23 Apr. 1720 (T.S.P.I., T.546, pp. 2-3).

[2] See ch. VII above.

[3] 29 Geo. II c. 24 (Ireland).

[4] *Rec. gen. syn.*, ii. 38.

[5] An account of this, as of the whole marriage question, is given in ch. XI below.

[6] 10 Geo. I c. 8 (Ireland). The act was passed in 1723 and was to remain in force for three years.

while the presbyterians, who failed to attain their object, were much more numerous and influential.[1] Quite possibly one reason for the success of the quakers was their political insignificance, which saved them from the jealousy of churchmen and landlords; but it seems equally likely that more attention would have been paid to the demands of the presbyterians, especially on such a question as marriage which, while of great importance to them, did not threaten the security of the established church, if they had been more firmly united. Some support for this view is to be found in a letter from William Conolly written just after the synod of 1723, at which feeling had run pretty high between subscribers and non-subscribers. The divisions of the dissenters, he says, will make them 'less considerable' in all matters.[2]

After these failures over the militia and marriages, the presbyterians made no further attempt to secure legislative relief till they returned to the attack upon the sacramental test. Before dealing with this renewed attack it is necessary to enquire how far the test was felt as a burden by the presbyterians at this time. Even before its imposition the number of them who became members of parliament was very small, a clear indication that their influence as landlords or as members of corporations was not extensive.[3] The imposition of the test excluded them completely from corporations and prevented those of them who were landlords from acting as justices of the peace. The former exclusion was undoubtedly felt as a serious grievance, at least in Belfast and Londonderry, in both of which the numbers and power of the dissenters were very considerable.[4] In Belfast, indeed, several presbyterian burgesses remained in office, neither taking the test nor carrying out their functions, until 1707, when they were obliged by parliamentary action to resign.[5] Even after this the presbyterians found means to make their influence felt in the town, to the great annoyance of the high churchmen, who complained of it to the English government: 'I must also acquaint your lordship that in Belfast the dissenting party have erected a society for the reformation of manners (as they call it) of which about fifteen are sworn once a month before the sovereign of the town in the nature of a

---

[1] On the question of presbyterian influence in the Irish parliament see ch. XIII below.

[2] Conolly to ——, 7 July 1723 (T.S.P.I., T.580, p. 22).

[3] Bp King to Bp Lloyd of Lichfield, 15 Dec. 1696 (Mant, *Ch. of Ire.*, p. 68): 'There were hardly ten dissenters in the house'.

[4] For Belfast see Benn, *History of Belfast*, p. 723, and below, pp. 141–2. For Londonderry see Reid, *History*, ii. 511, and above, ch. II.

[5] Abp King to Southwell, 8 Nov. 1707 (Mant, *Ch. of Ire.*, p. 186); *Commons' jn. Ire.*, iii. 391.

grand jury.... This society have taken upon them to compel the constables to go round the town with them, and to enter people's houses and take what persons they think fit and imprison them; their foreman was indicted last assizes for false imprisonment and fined, and the rest will be dealt with in the same manner if they continue to exercise such an arbitrary and illegal power'.[1] In 1718 the synod of Ulster recorded a complaint against the printing of 'obscene ballads' in Belfast and ordered that the printers should be advised against issuing such papers for the future.[2] Unofficial influence of this sort, however, even when unaccompanied by danger, was no substitute for legal power; and in striving for the removal of the test the presbyterians must have been looking forward especially to recovering their lost positions on the corporations of Belfast and Londonderry.

The exclusion from the magistracy can hardly have been so serious. Reid brings forward contemporary evidence to show that the number of magistrates who resigned as a result of the test act was very large.[3] But his witnesses are an English whig (Defoe) and three Irish presbyterian ministers, none of them likely to be impartial. Evidence of another sort appears during the dispute over commissions in the militia in 1716. Henry Maxwell of Finneybrogue, who had been M.P. for Bangor in Queen Anne's reign, wrote: 'The body of our dissenters consist of the middling and meaner sort of people, chiefly in the north, and in the north there are not many of them estated men when compared with those of the established church, so that when their disabilities shall be taken off their want of fortune and interest will always hinder them from coming into the militia in any invidious or dangerous numbers ...'[4] In the same letter, and apparently on the same grounds, he declares that the proposed admission of the protestant dissenters to commissions in the army 'would do the established church no real hurt and the dissenters not much good'. Maxwell was no enemy to the presbyterians (he was one of a committee of four appointed in 1704 to draw up heads of a bill for the relief of protestant dissenters[5]), and though in this letter he seems to be trying to prove a case, there is no reason to doubt the substantial accuracy of his statements. Sixteen years later, Primate Boulter represented the state of affairs in a very similar light: 'I am pretty well satisfied that the dissenters have very much magnified their importance here. Their strength is principally in the north, where

---

[1] Sir Constantine Phipps to lord treasurer, 26 Dec. 1712 (*Portland MSS*, v. 255).

[2] *Rec. gen. syn.*, i. 479. [3] Reid, *History*, ii. 512.

[4] Maxwell to ——, 9 Apr. 1716 (T.S.P.I., T.448, p. 280).

[5] *Commons' jn. Ire.*, iii. 135.

indeed they are numerous, but not the proprietors of much land or wealth. I have been assured that if the test were taken off there are not twenty persons amongst them qualified for substance to be justices of the peace'.[1] Supporting evidence of the small number of great landowners among the presbyterians might be deduced from the important part played in their councils by Colonel Upton of Templepatrick, who seems to have been without a rival amongst them. But even if the number of presbyterian landlords was greater than this evidence indicates, it has already been shown that there was one direction at least in which the sacramental test seems to have been ignored with impunity—the holding of commissions in the militia. As for those minor positions to which men of middle class could aspire, they were not likely to be secured, in the circumstances of those times, without more influence than the presbyterians possessed; and in Ulster where that influence was strongest such positions were not numerous.[2]

But though it might be considered proved that the number of presbyterians directly affected by the provisions of the test clause must have been very small, the fact remains that it was felt, whether reasonably or not, as a serious grievance. For some years after the disappointment of 1719 the matter was allowed to rest. But in 1722 the synod of Ulster drew up an address to the king, in which they complained of 'the discouragement and incapacities under which some of us lie, and by which we are distinguished from your other protestant subjects'.[3] An undated petition from the protestant dissenters of the south dwells much more explicitly on the evil consequences of the test upon the protestant interest in Ireland.[4] It is not likely that petitions alone would have accomplished very much. But about this time the government was compelled to pay attention to the position of the protestant dissenters, owing to the alarming growth of emigration, which affected them more closely than any other section of the population. The beginning of this emigration in 1717 has already been referred to. All commentators agreed that the emigrants were exclusively protestant.[5] Archbishop King tried to make

[1] Abp Boulter to Newcastle, 15 Jan. 1732 (T.S.P.I., T.722, p. 13).

[2] Baron J. Wainwright to Lord ——, 16 Jan. 1734 (T.S.P.I., T.756, p. 7). He speaks of the positions which would be opened to the Ulster presbyterians by the removal of the test as 'the little employments of the excise and customs'.

[3] Rec. gen. syn., ii. 37–8.

[4] T.S.P.I., T.659, p. 20. The original is along with papers of 1727. A reference to emigration makes it almost certain that it belongs to this period.

[5] E.g. Abp King to Abp Wake of Canterbury, 6 Feb. 1718 (C. S. King, A great archbishop of Dublin, p. 207); Boulter to Newcastle, 16 July 1728 (Boulter letters, i. 251). Wodrow to Colman, 30 Jan. 1730, implies the same thing (Wodrow correspondence, iii. 455).

out that they included as many churchmen as dissenters;[1] but the judges of assizes for the north-west circuit in reporting on the causes of the emigration in 1729 stated clearly, 'Most of those who leave the kingdom are protestant dissenters'.[2] In such a general movement spread over such a considerable period there is bound to be room for conflict of views, but the statement of the judges and the repeated opinion of the protestant dissenters themselves make it reasonably certain that they were the people principally concerned in the matter. This conclusion naturally gives rise to two questions. First, was the sacramental test a main reason for the large-scale emigration? Secondly, was the attempt to repeal the test made between 1731 and 1733 and sponsored by the government due in any measure to a desire to check this emigration?

To the first question an emphatic negative is given by H. J. Ford. Speaking of this period he says: 'Ulster emigration upon any important scale is to be attributed to economic and not to religious causes'.[3] Undoubtedly important economic causes of emigration did exist. In 1718 and 1719 Archbishop King laid stress on the destruction of Irish trade by the English parliament and on excessive rents as the main causes of the emigration just then beginning.[4] Both these causes are mentioned by later writers. In 1722 William Conolly describes the country as being in a miserable condition 'having neither money nor trade'.[5] Primate Boulter, having mentioned the emigration, goes on, 'the least obstruction in the linen manufacture, by which the north subsists, must occasion great numbers following'.[6] In another letter Boulter lays the responsibility on the landlords, who demand high rents.[7] Though Boulter's evidence alone might be of little value on this point, since he is trying to prove that the poverty of the farmers is not due to tithes, it is borne out by two other correspondents writing about the same time, both of whom attribute the increase in emigration to the raising of rents.[8] Almost ten years later Swift makes the same charge

[1] Abp King to Abp Wake of Canterbury, 2 June 1719 (Mant, *Ch. of Ire.*, p. 331).

[2] T.S.P.I., T.659, p. 74.

[3] H. J. Ford, *The Scotch-Irish in America*, pp. 167-8.

[4] Abp King to Abp Wake of Canterbury, 6 Feb. 1718 (C. S. King, *A great archbishop of Dublin*, p. 207); same to same, 2 June 1719 (Mant, *Ch. of Ire.*, p. 331).

[5] Conolly to Delafaye [?], 1 Mar. 1722 (T.S.P.I., T.546, p. 52).

[6] Abp Boulter to Newcastle, 16 July 1728 (*Boulter letters*, i. 251).

[7] Same to Bp Gibson of London, 13 Mar. 1729 (ibid., i. 289).

[8] Thomas Whitney to ——, 27 July 1728; Thomas Wyndham to ——, 11 Jan. 1729 (T.S.P.I., T.659, pp. 52-3, 64).

against the landlords and especially against the Irish Society.[1] Another, though a temporary, economic cause of emigration was a series of bad harvests which apparently led to serious scarcity.[2] In November 1728 Boulter produced a scheme for keeping down the price of corn.[3] But this did not achieve its object, for in the following spring he wrote, 'The scarcity of provisions certainly makes many quit us'.[4] In the same year the judges of the north-east and north-west circuits, reporting on emigration, declared that a good harvest 'may contribute very much to abate this humour in the people'.[5] Another reason for accepting the contention that economic and not religious causes were behind the emigration is to be found in the character of the emigrants. They were predominantly farmers, a class which would be affected by the sacramental test only in the most indirect way. On the other hand the presbyterians themselves persistently attributed the emigration to their religious grievances. In at least one memorial they complained of the effect of tithes, especially as collected by tithe farmers, and of the expensiveness of the spiritual courts which were used for their recovery. In the same document they alleged as other causes of emigration the interference which they suffered in conducting their schools, prosecutions on account of marriages, and the sacramental test.[6] In regard to marriages and schools Boulter writes, 'I told them that for some time they had not been molested about their marriages, and that as to their schoolmasters I was sure they had met with very little trouble on that head, since I had never heard any such grievance so much as mentioned till I saw it in their memorial'.[7]

The judges of the north-west circuit give a similar account. They admit that tithes are rigorously collected by tithe-farmers, but go on, 'As most of those who leave the kingdom are protestant dissenters, they complain of the discouragement put upon them by the test act, but in the counties we passed through we did not hear of any prosecutions against them upon that, or any other penal laws'.[8] The similar com-

[1] Swift to Barber, 30 Mar. 1737 (*Swift correspondence*, v. 429–30).

[2] *P.R.I. rep. D.K. 30*, p. 52; Thomas Wyndham to ——, 11 Jan. 1729 (T.S.P.I., T.659, p. 64).

[3] Abp Boulter to Newcastle, 23 Nov. 1728 (*Boulter letters*, i. 260).

[4] Abp Boulter to Newcastle, 13 Mar. 1729 (ibid., i. 288).

[5] T.S.P.I., T.659, p. 73.

[6] This account of the presbyterian memorial is taken from Boulter's letters. There is no mention of it in T.S.P.I. or in *Rec. gen. syn.* Abp Boulter to Carteret, 8 Mar.; to Newcastle, 13 Mar.; to Bp Gibson of London, 13 Mar. 1729 (*Boulter letters*, i. 285, 288, 289).

[7] Abp Boulter to Bp Gibson of London, 13 Mar. 1729 (ibid., i. 289).

[8] T.S.P.I., T. 659, p. 74.

plaint made by the protestant dissenters of the south has already been referred to.[1]

At first sight it might seem impossible to reconcile these conflicting statements. The presbyterians declared that they went to America to escape persecution. Most other contemporary evidence goes to show that such persecution was of little importance, and that the main causes of the emigration were economic. The truth probably is that both explanations are right, at least in part. No doubt the first large-scale emigrations were caused by economic conditions in Ulster. But as communications with North America became more frequent[2] presbyterians must have been strongly attracted by a land in which they would be not merely, as in Ireland, grudgingly tolerated but welcomed as equals. Once the alarm of the government had been aroused it was natural that the presbyterians in their anxiety to secure similar equality at home should point to this as their main reason for leaving Ireland.

The second question follows directly from the first. Was the government influenced by the presbyterian argument that the sacramental test was the cause of emigration when in 1731 it began to work for its repeal? While it is impossible to give an unqualified answer, three circumstances suggest that a negative is probably correct. First, as has already been pointed out, official opinion at the time was opposed to the presbyterian argument. Secondly, a considerable period passed between the judges' inquiry into the causes of emigration and the first suggestion that the government intended to make any move to repeal the sacramental test. Thirdly, the dissenters themselves refrained from using this occasion to make a concerted effort for repeal. Wodrow gives an account of this : 'The state of the dissenters in Ireland is lamentable enough. The great numbers of them who have of late come over in shoals to America have alarmed the government. This weakens the English interest and strengthens that of the Irish papists. This was thought might have been a proper season to get somewhat done for the easing our brethren's grievances there, especially the scandalous abuse of our Lord's ordinance by the sacramental test, which was one considerable incitement to them to come to America. The north and south, subscribers and non-subscribers, agreed to make an application to the parliament now sitting in Ireland for the removal of that burden. It was thought proper, however, to advise with their friends at London. For what reason I cannot tell, but they advised to waive this proposal. This is done and the time is

[1] See above, p. 87.

[2] For the influence of American agents in Ulster see Ford, *Scotch-Irish in America*, pp. 190 ff.

not yet come to build the Lord's house'.[1] When the presbyterians did renew the pressure for the repeal of the test in 1731[2] there is no evidence that either they or the English government, which about the same time began to work for the same end,[3] were concerned to put a stop to emigration. Nevertheless, it was probably the fact that the emigration question had called public attention to their grievances, together with the temporary settlement of their internal quarrels,[4] which decided the presbyterians to make a new move for relief.

This new move, the last serious attack on the sacramental test for almost fifty years, began in 1731, when the presbyterians sent a delegate to London.[5] Apparently opinion there was prepared for some sort of action. In December 1731 Walpole wrote to the duke of Dorset, who had just gone over to Ireland as lord lieutenant, that the time for relief to the Irish protestant dissenters had come, that in England such relief was considered 'universally right', and had the approval of the king and queen. Walpole suggests that the relief could be given by a clause added to one of the Irish bills then being considered by the English privy council, and goes on, 'It is represented to us that the house of lords will be very desirous of passing such a bill, and in the house of commons the opposition will be much less than was ever apprehended upon a like consideration'. Walpole explains that the government does not wish to act until Dorset's opinion is known;[6] but probably more importance was attached to that of Primate Boulter, communicated to Newcastle a fortnight later: 'I have made it my business to enquire of some of the lords and of some who best know the disposition of the house of commons, and I have reason to believe that if the repealing the test were to be attempted originally either in the house of lords or commons it could miscarry; but that if it comes over from England added to some Irish bill, it is still more certain of miscarrying'. He thinks that a majority both of bishops and of temporal lords will oppose it, while in the house of commons, where the dissenters think that government support might secure them a majority, even office-holders cannot be counted on to support the crown. 'And I am assured that when this

---

[1] R. Wodrow to Colman, 30 Jan. 1731 (*Wodrow correspondence*, iii. 456).

[2] *Rec. gen. syn.*, ii. 168; —— to Boulter, 6 Jan. 1732 (T.S.P.I., T.722, pp. 7-8).

[3] Walpole to Dorset, 30 Dec. 1731 (*Stopford-Sackville MSS*, i. 147).

[4] Though the general synod of 1726 resulted in the formal division of Irish presbyterianism, it produced a temporary abatement in the bitterness of internal controversy. See pp. 98-9 below, and Reid, *History*, iii. 205 ff.

[5] *Rec. gen. syn.*, ii. 168.

[6] Walpole to Dorset, 30 Dec. 1731 (*Stopford-Sackville MSS*, i. 147).

very thing was attempted under the duke of Bolton, after being recommended to the parliament from the king, not above ten out of fifty in places voted for the repeal of the test. . . .' His conclusion is, '. . . if any attempt in favour of the dissenters be thought proper, they should be directed to make the best interest they can against another session; and if they meet with encouragement try for a bill in the house of commons'.[1]

A few days after the dispatch of this letter a conference was held in Dublin at which the duke of Bolton, the chancellor and the speaker of the house of commons were present. Here it was finally decided that no bill from England containing a clause to remove the sacramental test could hope to pass. Later this decision was communicated to some of the leaders of the protestant dissenters, who were 'fully persuaded that the thing could not be done now at least'.[2]

The English government, though very much disappointed, would not press the matter in face of these opinions. But Newcastle could not forbear a caustic comment: 'It is indeed very extraordinary that such a clause should be liable to meet with difficulties in either house in a country where no distinction should be kept up among protestants which might be an occasion of disuniting them, considering the great disproportion in number that there is between them and the papists'.[3] But though the conduct of the parliament might be extraordinary, that of the Irish government was quite natural. Their business was to get the session over as quietly as possible and secure the voting of adequate supplies. These ends would not be forwarded by trying to push through an unpopular measure, especially if it were done by means of 'tacking'. Even the rumour of an attempt to repeal the test had produced a threatening situation: 'The apprehensions raised about the test have drawn more members to town than usual, and your experience will tell you that when they are together they are apt to give themselves and the government more trouble than could be wished'.[4]

The attempt to secure relief from parliament was not renewed until 1733, but in the interval a bitter pamphlet war was carried on. In this conflict Dean Swift took a leading part. Early in 1732 Boulter, dealing with the apprehensions aroused by the proposed repeal of the test, wrote, 'I find Dean Swift has begun already to sound the alarm'.[5] But the first move had been made by the other side and in the previous year when John Abernethy, a leading presbyterian minister in Dublin,

[1] Abp Boulter to Newcastle, 15 Jan. 1732 (T.S.P.I., T. 722, pp. 10 ff.).
[2] Same to same, 18 Jan. 1732 (ibid., pp. 15 ff.).
[3] Newcastle to Abp Boulter, 5 Feb. 1732 (ibid., pp. 25–26).
[4] Cary to Delafaye, 22 Feb. 1732 (T.S.P.I., T.722, p. 40).
[5] Abp Boulter to Newcastle, 15 Jan. 1732 (ibid., p. 13).

published *The nature and consequences of the sacramental test considered, with reasons humbly offered for the repeal of it*.[1] In the following year two pamphlets were issued under Swift's name.[2] One of these, originally printed as a broadside, is entitled *Queries wrote by Dr. J. Swift in the year 1732*. This is simply a short statement of the principal arguments in favour of maintaining the privileged position of the established church, put in the form of questions. The other is more elaborate and is a direct reply to Abernethy's pamphlet, *The advantages proposed by repealing the sacramental test impartially considered*. Next year he followed this up with another answer to Abernethy, *The presbyterian plea of merit in order to take off the test, impartially examined*.[3] In this pamphlet Swift answers the two main presbyterian arguments, that the repeal of the test was, first, a just reward for past services, and secondly, a necessary defence against the Roman catholic majority. To this latter point he returns, not with argument but with abuse, in a verse tirade, also belonging to 1733, *On the words brother-protestants and fellow-christians*, the moral of which is in the last two lines:

> 'For he that has so little wit
> To nourish vermin, may be *bit*'.

While this was going on in Ireland an attempt was being made in England to secure parliamentary relief for the English protestant dissenters, and Swift assumed that this would be followed by an attempt to do the same thing in Ireland.[4] The effort in England failed, but the project in favour of the Irish protestant dissenters was not abandoned. The duke of Dorset returned to Ireland in September 1733[5] with instructions to carry the repeal of the test if possible.[6] According to Swift's correspondent, Ford, the dissenters had received a definite promise that the test would be repealed in the approaching session of parliament.[7] When parliament opened in October the lord lieutenant urged the need for unity among protestants,[8] and though this elicited no response from

---

[1] Dublin, 1731.

[2] *Prose works of Jonathan Swift*, ed. Temple Scott, iv.

[3] There was formerly some doubt about the date of this pamphlet (see *Prose works of Jonathan Swift*, iv. 25–8), but the question is settled by a letter from Swift to Forde, 20 Nov. 1733 (*Letters of Jonathan Swift to Charles Ford*, ed. D. Nichol Smith, pp. 159 ff.).

[4] Swift to Ford, 9 Dec. 1732 (*Letters of Swift to Ford*, p. 144).

[5] *Liber mun. pub. Hib.*, i, pt. ii, p. 11.

[6] Abp Boulter to Newcastle, 18 Dec. 1733 (*Boulter letters*, ii. 108 ff.).

[7] Ford to Swift, 6 Nov. 1733 (*Swift correspondence*, v. 38).

[8] *Commons' jn. Ire.*, iii. 202–3.

either house it probably encouraged the representatives of the presby-terians who had come up to Dublin to press their case.[1] They were sanguine of success, and though Boulter was doubtful, Swift's opinion, even allowing for some exaggeration, shows that they must have had solid grounds for hope. In November 1733 he wrote to Ford: 'It is reckoned that the test will be repealed. It is said that £30,000 have been returned from England, and £20,000 raised here from servants, labourers, farmers, squires, whigs, etc. to promote the good work. Half the bishops will be on their side. . . . But we all conclude the affair desperate. For the money is sufficient among us to abolish Christianity itself. All the people in power are determined for the repeal, and some of your acquaintances, formerly tories, are on the same side'.[2] But Swift overestimated the danger. Less than a month later Boulter and Dorset were sending to England long apologies for their failure to carry out the wishes of the English government in the matter.[3] From these it simply appears that the opposition in the commons proving stronger and more determined than had been expected, the government, as in 1731, persuaded the dissenters that the best thing to do was to drop the pro-ject for the time being, though Dorset, according to his own account, promised them that if they thought fit to persist in bringing in a bill he would give them his full support both in his public and in his private capacity. However, 'they at last agreed to drop it as an attempt that could do them no service at present and might be of prejudice to them hereafter'.

The truth seems to be that once again the protestant dissenters were sacrificed to the convenience of the Irish government. The introduction of the relief bill was put off until the important business of the session had been got over. It was hoped that after this many of those opposed to the bill would go home. But the commons, afraid of the matter being forced through in a thin house, fixed a date beyond which no amend-ments to any of the acts to prevent the growth of popery would be received.[4] Thus the matter was forced to a decision and the government drew back. In Boulter's words, 'It was thought a very dangerous step to unite a majority of the house in an opposition to the intentions of the

[1] Abp Boulter to Bp Gibson of London, 1 Nov. 1733 (*Boulter letters*, ii. 107).

[2] Swift to Ford, 20 Nov. 1733 (*Letters of Swift to Ford*, pp. 160–1).

[3] Dorset to Newcastle, 14 Dec. 1733 (T.S.P.I., T.722, pp. 104 ff); Abp Boulter to Newcastle, 18 Dec. 1733 (*Boulter letters*, ii. 108 ff.). The account which follows is based on these two letters.

[4] It will be remembered that the sacramental test was originally imposed as part of an 'Act to prevent the further growth of popery' (2 Anne c. 6).

government'. Outside parliament, too, the opposition was growing: 'If the prudence of the prime serjeant had not stopped it, we should have had such a hurricane of addressing upon this subject, as you had about the excise'.[1] Such a recent example of the force of popular prejudice was not likely to be ignored; and whether Dorset's offer of full support was genuine or not, it seems clear that the dissenters were either cajoled or coerced into giving up their present hopes chiefly in order to save the government from a difficult situation. At the same time, of course, it must be recognised that by December 1733 no relief bill, even with government backing, had much chance of success. The most reasonable complaint against the conduct of the Irish government is that stated and countered by Boulter:[2] 'I find some of the dissenters now say the thing ought to have been tried sooner in the session. But as I mentioned before, it was the opinion of his majesty's servants that the supplies ought to be secured before any danger was run of raising heats in the house'. But Boulter's explanation simply shows once more that the interests of the dissenters were subordinated to the convenience of the government. Ultimately, of course, the responsibility for the maintenance of the test rested on the house of commons, who seem, in spite of presbyterian calculations, to have been almost unanimous against repeal. Their reasons were no doubt what they had always been. 'The truth is the gentlemen here are hearty friends to the constitution both in church and state, faithful to the protestant succession, and fond of the established religion, which they think a necessary bulwark against popery, and are not to be persuaded that their strength will be increased by opening the door to receive dissenters into the fortress'.[3]

This contempt of the Irish gentry for the alliance of the protestant dissenters, so different from the hearty co-operation which had existed during the revolutionary period and from the open confession of community of interest made during the invasion scare of 1715–16, arose in part at least from the confidence they felt in their ability to look after themselves. The long peace had made the fear of invasion a mere memory, and the Roman catholics, against whom the English government and the protestant dissenters alike urged the need for unity, had already sunk so far under the penal system as to seem incapable of arousing apprehension in the ruling class.[4] Yet this was the one argument which might have been powerful enough to overcome the average

[1] Baron J. Wainwright to Doddington, 2 Jan. 1734 (*Var. Coll.*, vi. 57).
[2] Abp Boulter to Newcastle, 18 Dec. 1733 (*Boulter letters*, ii. 108 ff).
[3] Baron J. Wainwright to Lord ——, 16 Jan. 1734 (T.S.P.I., T.756, p. 7).
[4] This is the point of view taken up by Swift in *The presbyterians' plea of merit* (1733). See p. 93 above.

Irish churchman's dislike of the protestant dissenters and lingering fear of presbyterian domination. Even in England where the protestant dissenters were a very small proportion of the population it proved impossible at this time to secure a complete repeal of the sacramental test. It is not then to be wondered at that in Ireland where they equalled or almost equalled the churchmen in numbers if not in wealth there should be a deep reluctance to admit them to any opportunity of wider political influence.

IX

THE LAST PHASE

The failure of the attempt to secure repeal of the test in 1733 was regarded by the presbyterians as putting an end to their hopes, at least for some considerable time. There is an air of finality about the terms in which the synod of 1734 resolved to wind up the account of the expenses incurred in the political activity of the previous years.[1] From this time onwards the question of the sacramental test fell completely into the background in the discussions of the general synod. It received casual half-hearted attention in 1737, when the synod ordered a letter to be written to their brethren in Dublin allowing them, in the synod's name, to address the lord lieutenant, 'and if they find it convenient to give a modest hint concerning the S.T.'.[2] But even this was exceptional. On subsequent occasions when the synod had reason to draw up loyal addresses no hint was given of any cause of discontent. The congratulatory address which followed the battle of Culloden was drawn up in consideration of the 'peace and liberty which the presbyterians enjoyed in Ireland'; and though at the same time they took note of the poverty of the country there is no mention of any religious persecution, nor even of tithes.[3] In 1756 a similar address laid even more emphasis on the 'civil and religious rights and liberties' which the presbyterians enjoyed.[4] In 1761 the address to the new king dwelt on the long and steady loyalty of the presbyterians to the house of Hanover, but did not suggest that they had anything more to ask for than the maintenance of existing conditions.[5] Twelve years earlier a leading presbyterian minister had summed up the attitude of his co-religionists in a sermon preached on the peace of Aix-la-Chapelle. Having spoken of the blessings of civil and religious liberty, he went on: 'And dissenters in particular, when they look back upon former times, and consider the hardships their forefathers suffered in every reign from the reformation to the revolution (or, should I say, the taking place of the Hanover succession) certainly have special reason to rejoice and be thankful for the freedom and tranquillity they enjoy'.[6]

[1] *Rec. gen. syn.*, ii. 197–8. [2] Ibid., ii. 230.
[3] Ibid., ii. 321–2. [4] Ibid., ii. 402–3. [5] Ibid., ii. 450–1.
[6] [G. Kennedy, jr.], *The great blessing of peace and truth in our days* (Belfast, 1749), quoted in T. Witherow, *Historical and literary memorials of presbyterianism in Ireland*, ii. 68–9.

While the presbyterians themselves were thus expressing their satisfaction with the existing state of affairs it is not surprising to find that no
effort was made to force relief upon them; and, in fact, for over forty
years the question of removing the sacramental test was left alone.
Various reasons combined to produce this long interval. In the first
place, though the statements of loyal addresses are not to be taken at
their face value, it seems clear enough that the presbyterians had little
to complain of. Prosecutions on account of marriages had ceased.[1]
Frequent indemnity acts lessened the effect of the sacramental test.[2]
These indemnity acts provide a problem. They would hardly have been
passed unless there were some to benefit by them. But if they were
effective they would surely have been mentioned during the controversy over the test in 1730–3. Both sides ignored them. The presbyterians argued as though the sacramental test were rigorously enforced;
the churchmen seemed to assume that it was and defended it on that
assumption. But whatever the circumstances in which the indemnity
acts were passed or the attitude of the various parties towards them,
they must have done something to ease the position of the presbyterians. This suggestion is supported by a letter which the Irish privy
council sent to the lord lieutenant along with an indemnity bill in
1760. They consider that it is necessary at that time so that persons
in office may, at the outset of the reign, be free from the fear of
penalties.[3]

Another, and more important, factor which weakened the demand
for the repeal of the sacramental test was the growth of divisions among
the presbyterians themselves on doctrinal questions. Up to 1726 the
Irish presbyterians had been divided into two unequal, but friendly,
bodies. By far the greater number adhered to the synod of Ulster; a few
congregations in Dublin and throughout the south and west, while
maintaining close and harmonious relations with the synod of Ulster
were not formally under its jurisdiction. In 1726 the synod excluded
from membership the non-subscribing presbytery of Antrim, and at the
same meeting set up a new presbytery in Dublin under its own control,
consisting of the subscribing ministers in the city and in various southern
towns.[4] Thus the split in the north was carried into the south; for the
remaining southern ministers formed themselves into a presbytery of

---

[1] See ch. XI below.

[2] See appendix to ch. VII above.

[3] Privy council of Ireland to lord lieutenant, 26 Nov. 1760 (*Cal. H. O. P.*,
1760–5, p. 6).

[4] *Rec. gen. syn.*, ii. 105, 108–9, 111. For the beginning of the subscription
controversy see ch. VIII above.

their own,[1] and this body co-operated closely with the presbytery of Antrim.[2] This double split in Irish presbyterianism opened the way for still further divisions. The unpopularity of the principles of the non-subscribers in Ulster and the suspicion that the synod was not whole-heartedly opposed to them disposed many people to welcome the ministrations of the seceders, who began to appear in Ireland as missionaries from Scotland in the seventeen-forties.[3] Not long after their establishment in Ireland the seceders broke into two antagonistic groups. So instead of two presbyterian bodies on friendly terms with each other, as at the beginning of the eighteenth century, there were now five,[4] among which most unfriendly relations sometimes existed. In spite of efforts to maintain co-operation for political and practical purposes, as in the address of 1761, and in the management of the widows' fund,[5] these divisions seriously weakened the influence of the presbyterians on Irish affairs and reduced their chance of securing further relief. Controversy took up a great part of their energies. Witherow lists 107 publications of all sorts by Irish presbyterian ministers between 1731 and 1775, and of these 49 are concerned with internal disputes on such questions as subscription, the position of the seceders etc.[6]

While bitterness between different sections of the presbyterians was increasing, relations between churchmen and protestant dissenters were becoming more friendly. In 1761, for example, the synod publicly thanked the primate for his aid in securing a charter for the widows' fund.[7] Such friendliness might be merely a matter of policy when shown by whig bishops, but when it appears in the everyday life of a parish clergyman it may be taken as representative of a new state of affairs. Thus we find Philip Skelton not only on the most intimate terms with the brother of the presbyterian minister of his parish,[8] but even helping the presbyterians to build a meeting-house in return for their assistance

[1] C. H. Irwin, *History of presbyterianism in Dublin and the south and west of Ireland*, p. 61.

[2] J. Armstrong, *History of the presbyterian churches in the city of Dublin*, p. 63.

[3] *Rec. gen. syn.*, ii. 330–1. The secession movement in Scotland arose in the seventeen-thirties and was the result of the reimposition of patronage upon the Scottish presbyterian church (Reid, *History*, iii. 240 ff.).

[4] The synod of Ulster (by far the most important); two bodies of non-subscribers, one in the north and one in the south; two bodies of seceders.

[5] *Rec. gen. syn.*, ii. 449, 459–60.

[6] T. Witherow, *Historical and literary memorials of presbyterianism in Ireland*.

[7] *Rec. gen. syn.*, ii. 448.

[8] S. Burdy, *Life of Philip Skelton* (1792; ed. 1914), p. 110.

in restoring the church.[1] Such an atmosphere would only be found where there was neither persecution on the one side nor resentment on the other.

But while ill-feeling between the church and protestant dissent was on the decline, social discontent steadily increased. The causes which had led to extensive emigration from Ulster to north America in the seventeen-twenties and thirties still remained.[2] These, and possibly the example of the agrarian outrages of the whiteboys in the south of Ireland, led to serious unrest in Ulster, directed partly at least against the exaction of tithes.[3] The oakboys, however, were not exclusively protestant dissenters, though the latter took an important part in the disturbances;[4] nor was their agitation connected with a demand for repeal of the sacramental test or any other improvement in the position of the presbyterians. The hearts of steel agitation, which arose some eight years later, even more clearly originated in agrarian grievances; and although tithes were once more brought forward as a ground of complaint, it is clear that they were of secondary importance.[5] In this latter movement the presbyterians were closely concerned, chiefly because they formed the majority of the tenants on the estates affected.[6] The presbyterian authorities tried to prevent violence, while at the same time drawing attention to the grievances which had provoked it.[7] But though the disorders were soon quieted the dissatisfaction of the people led to a rapid increase in emigration.[8]

Though the sacramental test was not at this time cited as one of the main grievances of the presbyterians, various circumstances were combining to increase their influence and to prepare the way for their emancipation. In 1768 the passing of the octennial act had brought Irish members of parliament into closer dependence upon the electors and so had increased the importance of the presbyterian voters of Ulster. The emigration which had followed the evictions on the Donegall

[1] Philip Skelton to William Knox, 6 May 1773 (*Var. coll.*, vi. 443–4).

[2] Emigration probably slackened during the colonial struggle with France, but certainly did not cease (*Laing MSS*, ii. 436).

[3] Burdy, op. cit., p. 145; W. Crawford, *History of Ireland* (1783), ii. 320; Halifax to lord lieutenant, 16 Dec. 1763 (*Cal. H. O. P., 1760–5*, p. 337).

[4] *Charlemont MSS*, i. 137; Abp Stone to Charlemont, 28 July 1763, (ibid., i. 141).

[5] Crawford, op. cit., ii. 323–6.

[6] Lecky, *Ire.*, ii. 50. The disturbances began as a result of evictions on the estate of Lord Donegall, near Belfast.

[7] Ibid., ii. 49 note; F. J. Bigger, *The Ulster land war*, pp. 151–3.

[8] Lecky, *Ire.*, ii. 51; Crawford, op. cit., ii. 326.

estates and the hearts of steel rising, though not directly attributable to religious persecution or discrimination, drew attention to the position of the presbyterians. The outbreak of the American war helped to bring the matter to a head. As the military situation became more critical the government could less and less afford to add to the number of its enemies or to lose a chance of making a new friend. The presbyterians of Ulster were looked upon as particularly dangerous from the republican nature of the principles which some at least of them were known to profess. Certainly their close connection with the recent emigration tended to identify them, in the government's view, with the rebellious element in America.[1] According to the bishop of Derry (the earl of Bristol), their desire for freedom from England was so great that they would even support a French invasion.[2] This is improbable. Dr Dickson, a noted presbyterian minister, preaching about the same time, urged a negotiated peace with the colonists as the keen desire of Irish presbyterians, but in reference to the possibility of a French invasion he was quite resolute: 'Should necessity call us forth to oppose the jealous enemies of our liberties and religion, we are ready to approve ourselves the steady friends of the constitution and the rights of our country'.[3] But the accuracy of the bishop of Derry's suspicion was of small moment beside the principle which he deduced from it: 'The rights of humanity demand a general and unlimited toleration at all times. Policy peculiarly requires it at present'. The repeal of the sacramental test, which would offend none but 'a few ignorant high churchmen', would, he argued, win the support of the presbyterians.[4] It was with this end in view that in 1778 a clause for repealing the sacramental test was added to heads of a bill for relief of Roman catholics sent over to England.[5] There was considerable doubt in Ireland about what would happen. If the bill came back without the clause the commons might refuse to pass it. But if it came back intact and passed the commons it might fail in the lords, owing to episcopal opposition.[6] The clause was removed in England, and the presbyterians had to wait another year for relief. As on previous

---

[1] Lords of the admiralty to secretary Conway, 17 Oct. 1765 (*Cal. H. O. P., 1760–5*, p. 611).

[2] Bp Hervey of Derry (earl of Bristol) to Lord George Germain, —— 1778 (*Stopford-Sackville MSS*, i. 249–50).

[3] 'The ruinous effects of civil war', a sermon preached at Ballyhalbert, 27 Feb. 1778, quoted in Witherow, op. cit., ii. 237.

[4] *Stopford-Sackville MSS*, i. 249–50.

[5] Lecky, *Ire.*, ii. 214; *Commons' jn. Ire.*, xviii. 463.

[6] General Irwine to Lord George Germain, 3 July 1778 (*Stopford-Sackville MSS*, i. 250–1).

occasions, suspicion of their principles made their alliance seem to involve more danger than it was worth.

Before long the position of the presbyterians was so greatly strengthened that their claims could no longer be overlooked with safety. In 1778 the threat of invasion and the inability of the government to provide for the safety of the kingdom led to the formation of volunteer companies in which from the beginning the presbyterians took a leading part. With such a force behind them it was quite natural that they should renew their demand for a concession which, had it been made freely in the previous year, would have been received as a generous gesture of friendship, but which was now looked upon as a natural right unjustly withheld. A one-sided, but not altogether unfair, view of the position is given by Philip Skelton, whose friendly relations with the presbyterians have already been noted: 'Under pretence of preparing to repel an invasion on this island, all sorts of protestants, but the dissenters most warmly, have taken up arms, which they now threaten to employ against England . . . just now I am told the trumpet of rebellion is loudly blown by the dissenting ministers of Ulster, and that, instead of thirty thousand, they boast of fifty thousand fighting men'.[1] While the forcible arguments at the disposal of the presbyterians and their friends thus increased, the position of the Irish government was made more embarrassing by their inability to afford adequate protection from American privateers. The depredations of the latter, however, did something to damp the republican ardour of the Ulster presbyterians who suffered under them.[2]

The policy of the government is only to be understood when the feverish excitement which the situation had aroused throughout the kingdom is realised. With the American war, the threat of invasion and the formation of the volunteers, a wave of nationalist feeling, often, and especially among the protestant dissenters, tinged with republicanism, had swept over the country.[3] Partly because of their own strength and influence, partly because of the apparent justice of their demand, the cause of the presbyterians was coupled with that of free trade in the course of action which the patriots urged on the government. The lord lieutenant (Buckinghamshire) saw that the removal of the sacramental test was necessary if the Irish government was to enjoy a period of security and peace. In December 1779 heads of a bill for

[1] Philip Skelton to William Knox, 30 Oct. 1779 (*Var. coll.*, vi. 447–8).

[2] James Callander to Lord George Germain, 18 Nov. 1779 (*Stopford-Sackville MSS*, i. 260–1).

[3] Lecky, *Ire.*, ii. 218 ff. The republicanism of the protestant dissenters is dwelt upon in the letter from James Callander mentioned above.

repealing the test were introduced into the Irish house of commons, passed unanimously, presented to the lord lieutenant[1] and, in spite of episcopal opposition in Ireland and pressure from the English government, transmitted to England.[2] While the bill was still under discussion there Buckinghamshire justified his transmission of it and his desire for its success in a private letter to Lord George Germain: 'Two or three letters from England have mentioned an intention to let our test bill pass. I know not the circumstances which would so much contribute to quiet the spirit of the most dangerous body in this kingdom as that measure's being fairly understood'.[3] Within a short time he was assured that the cabinet was likely to approve his measures,[4] and this presumably included one on which he had laid such stress. But that the struggle was not yet over is evident from the efforts still made by the high church party to secure the rejection of the measure. Archbishop Fowler of Dublin drew a doleful picture of the state of the church in Ireland if it should pass: '. . . our religion would not remain many years the established one in Ireland, and if they [the dissenters] adhere to their ancient tenets will not be even tolerated'.[5] It appears from his letter that the bill was still in England and that its final form had not yet been decided. But less than a week later the bishop of Derry wrote to the speaker of the house of commons (who was presumably in Dublin), 'Pray write me three lines to Derry to inform me if there will be any opposition to the repeal of the test act in our house'.[6] This would imply that the return of the bill was already regarded as certain, and the following month (March 1780) it arrived back in Ireland.[7] Opposition was now useless, and the measure passed into law.[8]

Thus after the struggle had been allowed to fall into abeyance for over forty years the Irish parliament secured for the presbyterians from an unwilling English government the very concession which that government had so often demanded in vain from that parliament's predecessors. The time and circumstances of the repeal provide a further illustra-

[1] Froude, *Ire.*, ii. 268 ; *Commons' jn. Ire.*, xix. 13, 115, 155.

[2] Froude, *Ire.*, ii. 268.

[3] Buckinghamshire to Lord George Germain, 10 Jan. 1780 (*Lothian MSS*, p. 360).

[4] Lord Macartney to Buckinghamshire, 21 Jan. 1780 (*Lothian MSS*, p. 361).

[5] Abp Fowler of Dublin to Lord George Germain, 5 Feb. 1780 (*Stopford-Sackville MSS*, i. 267–8).

[6] Bp Hervey of Derry (earl of Bristol) to Pery, 11 Feb. 1780 (*Buckinghamshire MSS*, p. 156).

[7] Lecky, *Ire.*, ii. 243 ; *Commons' jn. Ire.*, xix. 280.

[8] 19 & 20 Geo. III c. 6; *Commons' jn. Ire.*, xix. 360.

tion of the nature of the relations of the Irish presbyterians with the government during the eighteenth century. That the house of commons, which had previously refused to buy the alliance of the presbyterians against the Roman catholics by admitting them to political equality, should now make this very concession at a time when no danger from the Roman catholics was apprehended, requires explanation. Part of this explanation may lie in the increasingly friendly relations between the presbyterians and the members of the established church. But this can hardly be all. It is not a slur on human nature to seek some personal or selfish motive for the change, and this may be found in the political circumstances of the time. The Irish commons had entered upon a great struggle with the British government. The whole question of the relations between the two parliaments was going to be brought up. In pressing its claims the Irish parliament would have no stronger allies than the volunteers, and among the volunteers the presbyterians were very powerful. Any means by which they could be bound to the national cause or rendered more considerable in the country was an advantage to the patriot party. The latter, then, through their representatives in the Irish parliament, brought forward and supported the repeal of the test not out of fear of the presbyterians, but as a matter of policy; and the English government, after some hesitation, accepted the proposal from an unwillingness to disoblige such a considerable section of the house of commons.

This leaves the problem of the changed attitude of the English government. The explanation here lies almost completely in the fact that the administrations which in the first third of the eighteenth century had urged the repeal of the test were whig; that which resisted the demand for repeal in 1778 and conceded it unwillingly in 1780 was tory. There may also have been on the part of the English government some genuine fear of the republican principles of the presbyterians and of their sympathy with the Americans;[1] but this in itself would not have been of sufficient force to decide policy.

In concluding this chronological survey of the period under review attention must be drawn once more to the striking inversion of the parts played by the English government and the Irish parliament. During the years when the legal position of the protestant dissenters was being decided, parliament stood firmly opposed to concessions which the English government as consistently urged. Yet in the end it was the

[1] Lord lieutenant (Harcourt) to Lord Rochford, 21 Aug. 1775. He encloses a letter from an unnamed correspondent describing in strong terms the pro-American attitude of the Irish protestant dissenters (*Cal. H. O. P.*, *1773–5*, p. 388).

English government which had to be forced, by the action of the Irish parliament, to grant concessions so long demanded in vain. This inversion corresponds with a remarkable contrast between the relations of the presbyterians with the government at the beginning and at the end of the period. At the very time when they were complaining most bitterly of the persecution under which they suffered they enjoyed the government's favour and some measure of protection; when the hostility of parliament had changed to warm advocacy of their rights, the government was opposed to their demands and jealously suspicious of their principles. But this discrimination on the government's part was misplaced. The nationalism which was to lead on to the Dungannon convention and Grattan's parliament was not confined to the presbyterians. The latter had, for the time, abandoned their distinctive position. The practical toleration which they now enjoyed made the special favour of the English government unnecessary. In the demand for free trade, which was the main point at issue between England and Ireland, they were probably more deeply concerned than any other section of the population. Their religious grievances having sunk into the background, and their economic interests being those of the patriot party, they were now Irishmen first, and their fellow-countrymen recognised their right to this position and the rights which should follow from it.[1] The relationship between the presbyterians and the government could no longer be treated in isolation, but had been temporarily merged in a larger issue; and the theme which has been followed through nine chapters at this point loses its individual existence.

[1] Lord Charlemont coupled the protestant dissenters with the churchmen as 'those real citizens of Ireland in whom her strength consists'. (*Charlemont MSS*, i. 137).

PART TWO
SPECIAL TOPICS

◆◆

X
REGIUM DONUM

Aconnected account, as far as it is possible to construct one, of *regium donum*, that is the royal grant paid to the Ulster presbyterians, is indispensable in tracing the relations between them and the government. The grant was paid even before legal toleration had been extended to protestant dissent in Ireland; and so its importance was far greater than its monetary value, since it involved a sort of semi-official recognition. The government could not logically acquiesce in the persecution of a sect which it was itself subsidising. But at the same time it must be noted that the grant was not made by the Irish government or parliament and does not represent their attitude to the presbyterians. Indeed throughout the reign of Queen Anne they worked persistently to have the payment stopped and achieved a temporary success in 1714. With this limitation, however, it can be said that a table of the amounts paid at various times to the Ulster presbyterians shows their progress in the favour of the government:

Date of grant	Amount[1]
1672	£600
1691	£1200
1718	£1600 plus £400 to the protestant dissenters of the south.
1784	£2600 plus £400 as above and £500 to the seceders.

A more detailed account of *regium donum*, especially of its origin and early history, will provide a useful commentary on the fluctuating fortunes of the Irish presbyterians. Charles II's grant of £600[2] had been suspended during the reign of James II. On his arrival in Ireland in 1690 William promised to renew the grant and to increase it to £800. Actually when the grant was made in the following year it was for £1200.[3] In

[1] *Report of the Presbyterian Historical Society of Ireland 1909*, app. See also R. Black, *Substance of two speeches delivered in the general synod of Ulster at its annual meeting in 1812* (Belfast, n.d.), p. 78.

[2] *Presbyterian loyalty*, pp. 383–4.

[3] Ibid., p. 397, where the royal letter authorizing the payment of the pension is printed.

making the grant the king said that it was a reward for the loyalty of the presbyterians. An additional reason is suggested in a letter from Sir Robert Southwell to the earl of Nottingham. He reckons that the £1200 will mean £15 for each presbyterian minister in Ulster, and goes on, 'as King James works by his priests, so these men will do like service to his majesty by uniting the people unto him and making a good report of things in Scotland'.[1] Even the enemies of the dissenters saw some good in the grant. Bishop King wrote to Bonnell, 'I do not think it amiss the presbyters be paid their sum out of the treasury, it is good to have their tongues under the king's girdle, 'twill lose them in time some of their ministers with their people if I know their temper right'.[2]

The original arrangement was that payment should be made quarterly out of the customs of the port of Belfast, the authority for the payment being the king's letter to the collector, and the first payments were made in this way.[3] But when the establishment of Ireland was placed on a more regular footing the pension was not included in the list and neither the collector nor the commissioners of revenue would make any further payments. A petition explaining the situation was sent to the queen (William was abroad) and though Sir Robert Southwell expressed doubt about its success[4] the lords justices were ordered to make a new grant by letters patent under the great seal.[5] This arrangement was not entirely satisfactory, for by the end of 1693 payment was a whole year in arrear. Lord Capel, however, always friendly to the presbyterians, backed up their petition,[6] and in March 1694 a warrant was issued for payment of all arrears.[7] No further break in the payments seems to have occurred during William's reign.[8] At the beginning of Anne's reign the grant was renewed.[9] Though the warrant for the letters patent to pass under the great seal of Ireland was not issued until 23 December 1702 the presbyterians were to lose nothing by the delay,

---

[1] Southwell to Nottingham, Belfast, 18 June 1690 (*Finch MSS*, ii. 301).

[2] Bp King to Bonnell, 26 June 1691 (King corr. T.C.D.).

[3] The receipt given to the collector by the ministers appointed to receive the payment is in Crosslé papers (P.R.O.N.I., T.780), p. 34. This is for payment of the first quarter; payment of the second quarter is noted in 'Payment and receipt book, revenue and army, Ireland' (P.R.O.N.I., T.689, p. 91).

[4] Southwell to Bp King, 8 June 1691 (King corr. T.C.D.).

[5] *Cal. S. P. dom., 1690–1*, p. 481. This contains the substance of the petition, as well as the queen's instructions to the lords justices.

[6] Capel to Shrewsbury, 15 Feb. 1694 (*Cal. S. P. dom., 1694–5*, p. 391).

[7] Ibid., p. 414.

[8] *Cal. S. P. dom., 1699–1700*, p. 203.

[9] Queen's Letter, 23 Dec. 1702 (Crosslé papers, P.R.O.N.I., T.780, p. 34).

for the grant was to date from the time of the last payment.[1] It is, however, doubtful if full payment was made at this time.[2]

This renewal of the grant seems to have been a matter of form carried through with little difficulty, though with some delay. But even before the renewal, complaints were being heard about the use to which the presbyterians were putting the money. According to Bishop King they used it to set up new congregations; and the fact that the fund was controlled by a group of ministers gave the latter considerable influence over their brethren, which was prejudicial to the government.[3] These complaints had no immediate effect. But King's attitude was shared by others and in the following year the Irish house of commons expressed itself even more strongly on the subject. Perhaps owing to its annoyance at the failure of some of the Ulster presbyterian ministers to take the abjuration oath, the commons passed a resolution in committee of the whole house 'that it is the opinion of this committee that the pension of £1200 per annum granted to the presbyterian ministers in Ulster is an unnecessary branch of the establishment'.[4] The temper of the commons appears from the fact that the resolution was virtually unanimous.[5]

Some of the presbyterians and their friends seem to have feared that this would cut off *regium donum* completely.[6] But though it failed to do this it put them on the defensive. They were especially concerned to show that the money received had been equally distributed, which would suggest that Bishop King's charges had had some publicity. To this end the agent responsible for distributing *regium donum* made a deposition in 1703 before a notary public that all payments were made equally, under the direction of the trustees and with full approval of the recipients.[7] This declaration was at best ambiguous. At the synod of 1702 it was decided that since the newly established congregation at Breaky and Kells could not support their minister he should receive, in addition to his regular share of *regium donum*, £20 in the first year, £15 in the second year, £10 in the third and subsequent years. At the same time it was revealed that *regium donum* had been used in an attempt to establish a minister in Galway. These extraordinary payments were apparently

[1] *Cal. S. P. dom., 1702–3*, p. 348.

[2] McCracken to Joshua Dawson, *c.* 1702, complaining that all arrears have not been paid (Crosslé papers, P.R.O.N.I., T.780, pp. 59–60).

[3] Bp King to Bp Ashe of Clogher, 24 Mar. 1702; to Southwell, 28 Mar. 1702 (Mant, *Ch. of Ire.*, pp. 125–7).

[4] *Commons' jn. Ire.*, iii. 62.

[5] Southwell to Nottingham, 21 Oct. 1703 (*Cal. S. P. dom., 1703–4*, p. 164).

[6] Samuel Ogle to [Robert Harley] 29 Apr. 1704 (*Portland MSS*, v. 82).

[7] Crosslé papers (P.R.O.N.I., T.780), p. 43.

made out of one quarter of the fund which was annually set aside for 'public uses'.[1] But though the charges made against them might have more foundation than the presbyterians were willing to admit, the attempts to have *regium donum* suspended failed. This failure was attributed by the presbyterians to the intervention of the duke of Ormond whom they addressed as follows, 'We return your grace our most humble hearty thanks for your late particular kindness in interposing your interest with her sacred majesty for the continuing her royal bounty towards us'.[2]

Apparently the money was paid without difficulty or important public opposition for several years. After the imposition of the sacramental test the ministers had some doubts about the legality of continuing to receive it, but these were soon set at rest.[3] This period of peace lasted until 1710. In June of that year *regium donum* appears in the list of pensions in the commons' journals and was apparently passed over in silence.[4] But in the following October and November the direction of affairs both in Ireland and in England fell almost entirely into the hands of the tories.[5] Next year the attack on the protestant dissenters was re-opened by the Irish house of lords who addressed to the queen a representation of the state of religion.[6] In this they dwelt especially upon the evils of *regium donum*: 'From this fund also we doubt not they have supplies to employ and maintain agents, support law-suits against the church, to form seminaries to the poisoning of the principles of our youth, and in opposition to the law, to set up synods and judicatories, destructive of your majesty's prerogative'. Convocation also took up the attack and they too concentrated on *regium donum*. Probably the high churchmen were aroused by the expansion of the presbyterians at this time and at the failure of their attempt to check it at Drogheda. Between 1690 and 1711 thirty-two new presbyterian congregations had been established, twenty-two of them since 1700. In spite of the efforts made at this time the expansion continued and by 1720 a further seventeen congregations had been set up.[7]

[1] *Rec. gen. syn.*, i. 62.

[2] Crosslé papers, p. 55. The address is undated, but probably belongs to 1704; it congratulates Ormond on his safe arrival, and he returned to Ireland in November of that year (*Liber mun. pub. Hib.*, i, pt. ii, p. 10).

[3] *Reg. gen. syn.*, i. 101 (synod of 1705).

[4] *Commons' jn. Ire.*, iii. 534.

[5] See ch. V above.

[6] *Lords' jn. Ire.*, ii. 410–11.

[7] These figures are compiled from *History of the congregations of the presbyterian church in Ireland*, ed. W. D. Killen (Belfast, 1886).

Some account of these attacks and of the presbyterian defence has already been given in chapter V. The government refused to suspend payment of *regium donum*, but the three most important of the presbyterian ministers who had refused to take the abjuration oath were excluded from the list of those to whom shares were to be paid for the Christmas quarter in 1712.[1] In the same year the demand for the stopping of the grant was taken up by the lords justices[2] and about the same time the excitement caused by the Belturbet affair served to reinforce their arguments. In spite of this it was not until 1714 that payment was suspended.[3]

The presbyterian synod of that year was held in Belfast in June and immediate action was resolved upon. Addresses were drawn up to the queen and the lord lieutenant setting out the grievances of the Irish presbyterians, and to reinforce these Francis Iredell, who had acted as their agent on previous occasions, was to be sent to London.[4] When he gave his report a year later the whole situation had been changed by the accession of the house of Hanover. He had been graciously received by the king, and the lord lieutenant had declared himself in favour of the presbyterian demands. The question of *regium donum* had been settled, apparently without difficulty, and there were hopes of its augmentation.[5] There was, however, no immediate increase in the amount, nor can it be ascertained exactly when the regular payments of the existing grant were resumed. From Iredell's report it would seem that the resumption was not earlier than the summer of 1715. The list of payments in the Irish treasury office shows that no arrears were due at Michaelmas 1715, and that payments were made in full from that date.[6] The figures given in this list are not entirely consistent, but taken together with the absence of any complaints by the presbyterians they indicate that in all probability the gap in the payments was made up at least from the accession of George I.

[1] Crosslé papers (P.R.O.N.I., T.780), pp. 40–1.

[2] Lords justices to Ormond (ibid., p. 53). The letter is undated, but is signed by Constantine Phipps and the archbishop of Tuam, who were lords justices from March 1712 to September 1713 (*Liber mun. pub. Hib.*, i, pt. ii, p. 10).

[3] See ch. V above.

[4] *Rec. gen. syn.*, i. 341.

[5] Ibid., i. 364 ff.

[6] T.S.P.I., T.519, pp. 76–7. From this it appears that for the year and three-quarters from Michaelmas 1715 to Midsummer 1717 the sum due to the presbyterian ministers was £2100, there being no arrears. The vice-treasurer, however, is stated to have paid £2400, and yet £600 arrears are put down as due at Midsummer 1717.

It is not easy to estimate exactly the financial importance of *regium donum* to the presbyterians, though it is obvious that it could not have sufficed for all the purposes to which their enemies said it was being put. In 1689 it was reckoned that there were about eighty congregations in Ulster.[1] If *regium donum* were evenly distributed each minister would receive £15, the amount estimated by Sir Robert Southwell.[2] No stipulation was made about such equal distribution. The original grant simply names a number of persons (all of them presbyterian ministers) to whom the money was to be paid 'to be by them distributed among the rest'.[3] In the records of the synod of 1702 appears a practice, apparently regularly followed, of setting aside one quarter of the money 'for public uses'.[4] The amount for distribution was thus reduced to £900. At the same time, the number of congregations was increasing; in 1702 it was 100, ten years later, 114. Even if the whole grant were evenly distributed each share would be little more than £10, the deduction would reduce it to about £8. This cannot have formed a very large proportion of a minister's income. The synod of 1702 seems to have regarded a local contribution of £40 as the minimum to make up a 'competent stipend'.[5] This was in a country parish and probably town congregations would be expected to give more. But even this, with a share of *regium donum*, would amount to more than was paid to the curates of many absentee incumbents. Goldsmith's parson of the mid-century was 'passing rich on forty pounds a year'. Nevertheless, the rapid increase in the number of congregations, and the attractive security of a government grant, explain the desire for an increase in *regium donum*.

This increase, expected in 1715, came in 1718. It is mentioned almost casually in the records of the general synod and there is no indication of any address of thanks.[6] Probably the presbyterians regarded the increase as a poor substitute for the legislative relief which they had expected since the change of dynasty. The most interesting thing about the new grant is that it was to be divided between the presbyterians of Ulster and the protestant dissenters of the south, who were now for the first time officially countenanced by the government. They were neither so numerous nor so well organised as their northern brethren and in their own strength could have accomplished little. Their inclusion in the

[1] Reid, *History*, ii. 590 ff.

[2] See above, p. 107.

[3] *Presbyterian loyalty*, p. 397.

[4] *Rec. gen. syn.*, i. 62.

[5] Ibid., i. 62.

[6] Ibid., i. 476. The reference is to a payment to be made 'out of the first additional *regium donum*'.

royal bounty was probably due in large measure to their co-operation with the synod of Ulster in the agitation for repeal of the test act which occupied the early years of the reign of George I. In this way their existence and claims were more forcibly brought before the English government.[1]

At first sight it might seem that this additional grant was intended as a sort of compensation to the Irish presbyterians for disappointments in other directions. It was made in 1718 when they were still agitating unsuccessfully for a legal toleration and the repeal of the sacramental test, and after they had been disappointed over the question of commissions in the militia and army. The grant was placed on the English instead of the Irish civil list as if it were intended to secure it against present opposition or future suspension at the hands of the high church party in Ireland. On the other hand the increase had been promised, or at least considered, since the beginning of the reign,[2] and its coming at this time may have been purely fortuitous. Certainly the Irish presbyterians did not regard it as a substitute for toleration, for which both they and the English government continued to work.

The subsequent history of *regium donum* is uneventful. The high church party dropped an agitation in which they could have no hope of success, and though the money was not always regularly paid[3] at least the constant threat of complete suspension was removed. On the other hand, the fact that part of a minister's income was received from the state was bound to produce a certain dependence upon the government, a result foreseen and counted upon by William III's advisers when the original grant was made.[4] There is, however, only the flimsiest evidence that the government ever took advantage of this dependence to interfere with the internal affairs of the synod of Ulster. In 1723 Wodrow reports a rumour that the synod of that year had been deterred from taking further proceedings against the non-subscribers by a message from the king threatening the removal of *regium donum*.[5] It is likely enough that

[1] See note at end of this chapter.

[2] *Rec. gen. syn.*, i. 364 ff. Memorials on the subject presented by the protestant dissenters both north and south in the first year of the reign were favourably received. They are referred to in a later petition in T.S.P.I., T.659, pp. 61–3. This is undated, and comes at the end of the papers of 1728; but since it states that no additional grant has yet been made it must belong to the period before 1718.

[3] There are petitions for arrears in 1738 and 1739 in Crosslé papers (P.R.O.N.I., T.780), p. 55.

[4] See above, p. 107.

[5] R. Wodrow to William Livingston, 29 Oct. 1723 (*Wodrow correspondence*, iii. 85).

the English government viewed with distaste any attempt to coerce the non-subscribers, not only because of its opposition to religious persecution, but also from the natural jealousy which any government might feel of the increasing strength of a possibly rival authority. But though on these general grounds the government might be willing to aid the non-subscribers there is no other evidence that it adopted this way of doing it and the action and attitude of the synod are easily explicable without assuming any outside intervention. It appears, however, that about this time some change in the method of distributing the additional grant made in 1718 was proposed and there were fears that this would place more influence in the hands of the non-subscribers and their English friends. But this change was not made and there is no suggestion that the original move was on the government's side.[1] On the contrary, the opinion of the Irish government was that the divisions of the presbyterians had the advantage of reducing their political influence, and that their dependence on the government was best secured by fair division of the royal bounty between both parties according to numbers and by giving both equal protection.[2] But even if, on this occasion, the government did attempt to influence the synod by threatening to withdraw supplies, there is no evidence that such an attempt was made again.

At the same time it is worth noting that the general synod of Ulster was itself able to employ *regium donum* to enforce its authority. At the synod of 1718 several presbyteries were threatened with suspension of their share of the grant if they did not pay sums applotted on them by the synod; and money in the treasurer's hands, due to the presbyteries of Belfast, Strabane and Derry as their shares of *regium donum*, was to be stopped for the payment of debts owed by them.[3] Later on, in 1734, the expenses involved in the move for the repeal of the test act were met, temporarily at least, out of *regium donum*.[4]

With the death of George I came the difficulty of having the additional grant renewed. The circumstances attending the renewal illustrate the improvement that had taken place since the death of Queen Anne in the position of the Irish presbyterians and in their relations with the leaders in the state and in the established church. In 1729 a deputation was sent to London to negotiate for a renewal of the payments, and this deputation was armed with a letter of introduction and recommendation from

---

[1] Reid, *History*, iii. 165–6, where the account is based on Wodrow's MS letters and his *Analecta*, iv. 232.

[2] William Conolly to ——, 7 July 1723 (T.S.P.I., T,580, p. 22).

[3] *Rec. gen. syn.*, i. 479–80.

[4] Ibid., ii. 196–7.

Primate Boulter to Sir Robert Walpole, a letter which may be regarded as sealing the alliance between the Irish presbyterians and the whig bishops.[1] But this alliance brought no further pecuniary gains to the presbyterians; George II renewed the grant but did not increase it. On at least two occasions the synod of Ulster considered the advisability of applying for an increase.[2] But either the application was not made, or if made met with no success and the amount paid remained the same until 1784.

This account of *regium donum* provides another example of the inconsistency and compromise into which the Irish government was forced in the seventeenth and eighteenth centuries (as well as at other periods) by the curious mixture of races and religions in the kingdom. The claims implicit in the presbyterian system, logically carried out, would have established it in Ulster as firmly as in Scotland. The laws of the kingdom of Ireland, until 1719, recognised but one church to which all were bound, under penalties, to conform. Neither the claims of the presbyterians nor the laws of the country could be completely ignored or completely carried out. So the existence of organised presbyterianism was connived at, and presbyterian ministers were paid by the government to perform functions which had been declared illegal by act of parliament. Even the passing of the toleration act did not entirely remove the inconsistency. First, presbyterian farmers were compelled to pay tithes for the maintenance of the anglican clergy, while the government, which professed to be anglican, was subsidising the presbyterian ministers. Secondly, while the established church, after the failure of its last serious attempt to secure some measure of independence in the reign of Queen Anne, was kept under strict state control, the presbyterian synod, though in the direct pay of the government, was left free to regulate its own affairs. But in spite of this inconsistency it is not altogether unreasonable to regard the policy of the government in this matter as a short and unconscious step towards the modern democratic principle that all religions have not only an equal right to freedom but an equal claim upon the state.

[1] Abp Boulter to Walpole, 31 Mar. 1729 (*Boulter letters*, i. 295).
[2] *Rec. gen. svn.*, ii. 307 (1744), 347 (1749).

NOTE

THE first extension of *regium donum* to the protestant dissenters of the south

IRWIN states that in 1708 the protestant dissenters of the south of Ireland received a grant of £800 from the English government.[1] This statement can be traced through Mathews,[2] whom Irwin gives as his authority, to Calamy. The last named is quite explicit. He says that *regium donum* was continued in Ireland from 1690 'with an addition in the reign of Queen Anne of eight hundred pounds per annum, for the south of Ireland, in which there are fewer meetings and fewer ministers than in the north. In soliciting for which I must own, that I myself very freely joined with worthy Mr Joseph Boyse (who was then in London) in an earnest application to my old acquaintance the earl of Sunderland for his interest'.[3]

But it must be noted that Mathews' account is entirely based on Calamy (and not accurately based, for he fixes the date, which Calamy leaves vague) and has no independent value. This story, then, rests on Calamy's statement alone. But Calamy makes no mention of the later grant of 1718. It seems, then, almost certain that, writing probably a considerable time after the event, he has antedated the grant of 1718 and confused the circumstances, misled, perhaps, by his participation in some previous deputation, in Queen Anne's reign, on behalf of the protestant dissenters of the south.

[1] C. H. Irwin, *History of presbyterianism in Dublin and the south and west of Ireland*, p. 28.

[2] G. Mathews, *Account of the regium donum*, p. 15.

[3] E. Calamy, *Historical account of my own life*, ed. J. T. Rutt, ii. 471–2.

XI

PRESBYTERIAN MARRIAGES

Of the various forms of inconvenience or persecution to which Irish presbyterians were subject in the eighteenth century none called forth such frequent complaints as the action taken against them in the church courts on account of their marriages. This was a matter which affected not only the ministers and their more prominent adherents, but every man and woman, however unimportant, who were married according to the presbyterian form, and it affected not themselves only but their children also. In the settlement of this grievance, therefore, every individual presbyterian had an interest. Yet in spite of this interest and of persistent effort it was a considerable time before effective legal redress was secured, and even until the nineteenth century settlements dependent upon marriages celebrated by presbyterian ministers might in certain circumstances be disputed at law.

This long delay was at least partly due to the fact that in the eyes of eighteenth century lawyers marriage was still a religious ceremony no less than a civil contract; and matters relating to it must be tried in the ecclesiastical courts. Any attempt to limit the jurisdiction of these courts would be regarded as an attack upon the rights and security of the church. Again, proceedings taken in connection with presbyterian marriages did not depend upon any penal statute, but upon the assumption made by the ecclesiastical lawyers that only marriages performed by episcopally-ordained clergy were valid. Presbyterian ministers who performed marriages were charged with having done so clandestinely in defiance of the civil and ecclesiastical law; persons so married were charged with fornication.[1] Relief would have to be given not by the removal of any statutory disability or penalty, but by the recognition of the equality, in respect of marriages, of the presbyterian ministers with the clergy of the established church, an act which would arouse the fury of the high churchmen. Furthermore, while the government could and did interfere to prevent penal laws which were still on the statute book from being enforced in the civil courts, it was more difficult to take similar action in the ecclesiastical courts. The latter were numerous, many of them in remote parts of the kingdom, the cases

---

[1] Specimens of these charges are printed in *A vindication of marriage as solemnized by presbyterians in the north of Ireland* (1702), pp. 43, 64. Marriages performed by Roman catholic clergy were regarded as irregular, but valid.

were petty, the persons involved obscure. There was little here to arouse public opinion or affect political parties. So while the act of uniformity was allowed to die, and while kings and their governments were making every effort to secure for the Irish presbyterians a legal toleration and repeal of the sacramental test, obscure men and women, who suffered no inconvenience from the lack of the former and who would have been in no way better off for the latter, continued to endure indignity, inconvenience and expense through having been married by their own ministers.

This form of attack upon the presbyterians appears to date only from the latter years of William III. A petition on the subject, bearing no date but almost certainly belonging to this period, declares: '. . . no minister of our profession hath till now of late ever been troubled on such account'.[1] The minutes of the presbytery of Antrim show that even during the reign of James II presbyterian ministers not only celebrated marriages but also, during part of the reign at least, publicly proclaimed the banns.[2] In spite of this previous toleration, however, one of the complaints made by Bishop Walkington of Down and Connor in his petition to the lords justices of England (1698) is this: 'They generally everywhere celebrate the office of matrimony, by which means the settlements made upon such marriages, and the titles of children to their inheritances, who are born of persons so joined together, are rendered disputable at law'.[3] It would seem that the bishop got little satisfaction; for next year the synod of Ulster advised ministers to marry any of their people who desired it. The same synod on the same day decided to draw up an address to the government, in which they asked for a continuation of 'exemptions from molestation on account of marrying', which would imply that so far the bishop's threats had not been put into force.[4]

The attack on presbyterian marriages having once begun soon spread. In 1699 Lord Galway, then one of the lords justices, reported that the bishop of Derry (King) was attacking the presbyterians on account of their marriages; but though he agrees that the presbyterians are in the wrong, they are so obstinate that moderation is necessary.[5] In the same

---

[1] The petition is printed in Reid, *History*, ii. 484 ff, where it is attributed to 1701. There is a transcript in P.R.O.N.I. (T.525) from which it appears that the original (Wodrow MSS,, f. 51, no. 48) is endorsed 'Probably *c*. 1708(?)'. This is clearly impossible; by 1708 prosecutions for marriages had been going on for several years.

[2] Minutes of the presbytery of Antrim (transcript in library of Presbyterian Historical Society, Belfast), pp. 366, 380 (1 Nov. 1687, 10 Jan. 1688).

[3] P.R.O.N.I., T.525.

[4] *Rec. gen. syn.*, i. 39.

[5] Galway to Vernon, 24 July 1699 (*Cal. S. P. dom., 1699–1700*, p. 241).

year the government seems to have suggested to the presbyterian ministers that they should stop celebrating marriages, but without success.[1] About the same time Bishop Ashe of Clogher entered upon a correspondence with the lords justices of Ireland, the object of which was to induce them to back up an episcopal campaign against presbyterian marriages. He announced the scheme in a letter to Bishop King in October 1699.[2] By the following January he was able to report a promise from the lords justices 'that some effectual course shall speedily be taken about marriages by dissenting ministers'.[3] A few weeks later he writes again on the same subject: 'I must needs say that in my neighbourhood the dissenting ministers are grown more modest than they were and of late send their people to our clergy to be married; however some declaration from the government is absolutely necessary'.[4] It is impossible to discover if this compliance on the part of presbyterian ministers was general. In view of the synod's decision of the previous year and of subsequent events it probably was not. As to the 'declaration' which the bishop hoped to get from the government, he waited in vain for it until 1701, and then considered it more prudent to defer the scheme until the arrival of the lord lieutenant.[5] The latter (Lord Rochester) arrived in the same year, but any hopes which the bishop may have had were destroyed by the adroitness of the presbyterians, who managed to get the whole question referred to the English government and eventually to the king.[6] As has already been pointed out, however, this was a matter in which the direct interference of the government was bound to be delayed; and though the bishops did not receive the official support they desired neither did the presbyterians get any immediate protection. The vigour with which the synod of 1701 laid down the rule that all parties to be married should be proclaimed beforehand 'on three several sabbaths', with the penalty of suspension for any minister who offended,[7] may have arisen from the fear of attack on the validity of their marriages. That such attacks had to be met is proved by the collections made to defray the expenses of those prosecuted.[8] There is evidence that such prosecu-

---

[1] George Lang, of Newry, to Wodrow, 23 Oct. 1699 (Wodrow's MS letters, i, no. 61; quoted in C. H. Irwin, *History of presbyterianism in Dublin and the south and west of Ireland*, p. 15 note).

[2] Bp Ashe of Clogher to Bp King, 28 Oct. 1699 (King corr. T.C.D.).

[3] Same to same, 12 Jan. 1700 (ibid.).

[4] Same to same, 24 Jan. 1700 (ibid.).

[5] Same to same, 1 June 1701 (ibid.).

[6] A full account of the transaction is given in Reid, *History*, ii. 484 ff.

[7] *Rec. gen. syn.*, i. 53.

[8] Ibid., i. 61.

tions increased about this time. Kirkpatrick's *Presbyterian loyalty*, in dealing with the year 1702, mentions 'numerous and violent prosecutions, in the spiritual courts, of many of untainted reputation, who were libelled and prosecuted as fornicators, merely for cohabiting with their own wives, whom they had married according to the presbyterian way'.[1] A number of pamphlets published in this and the following years now serve to indicate the bitterness of the dispute, and no doubt served then to increase it.[2] At the same time, it must be noted that these prosecutions were not always speedily successful. At Magherafelt, for instance, a presbyterian minister intruded into the parish and married a couple in a public ale-house. This was reported to Bishop King in November 1700;[3] but although a prosecution was started against the offender he was still at large in the following February, had married another couple in the interval, and apparently expected the English government to put a stop to any proceedings against him.[4]

This increase in the number of prosecutions on account of marriages came at a bad time for the presbyterians. In March 1702 King William died and they made no secret of the fact that they regarded this as a disaster for their cause. 'As to the dissenters of Ireland, they seem to be in great fear, and nothing could show more clearly the interest they thought themselves to have in his late majesty's favour, than the dejection that appears amongst them at present'.[5] So wrote Bishop King to Sir Robert Southwell. In the same letter he indicates that Irish churchmen were preparing to take advantage of the change in the government and it was ominous for the presbyterians that among other examples of their insolence he mentions their celebrating marriages. The new reign, however, brought the Irish presbyterians new grievances—the abjuration oath, the sacramental test, the attempt to take away *regium donum* —so that the question of marriages fell into the background. But though little is heard of it for the first ten years of the reign there is no reason to suppose that prosecutions ceased. About 1712, however, they seem to have been pressed with added vigour. The signal for this was probably the action taken by convocation, which in 1711 passed a canon for the prevention of clandestine marriages, so worded as to include all

[1] p. 507. For an account of *Presbyterian loyalty* see above, p. 58.

[2] The most important of these pamphlets are: *A vindication of marriage as solemnized by presbyterians in the north of Ireland* (1702); E. Synge, *An answer to a vindication of marriage* (1704); *A defence of the established church and laws in answer to a book entitul'd A vindication of marriage* (1705).

[3] Thomas Lawson to Bp King, 30 Nov. 1700 (King corr. T.C.D.).

[4] Same to same, 1 Feb. & 15 Feb. 1701 (ibid.).

[5] Bp King to Southwell, 28 Mar. 1702 (Mant, *Ch. of Ire.*, pp. 126–7).

marriages save those performed by clergy of the established church.[1] This renewed campaign seems to have had some effect. In 1712 William Haire of Longford reported to Wodrow: 'We of the presbyterian persuasion in this kingdom do yet enjoy our liberty, though there are many of our ministers that are troubled and persecuted in the bishops' courts for marriages, so that most of our people do marry according to the rites of the established church to prevent danger'.[2] A representation to the earl of Oxford in the following year produced no immediate result.[3] But though no assistance was received from the government, temporary relief was sometimes secured by application to the civil courts, as appears from the synod records of 1714: 'Whereas Mr. Samuel Smith jr. and John Kyle, both of Belfast, have applied to the interloquitur of this synod, representing that both of them have been under a severe and chargeable prosecution, in the ecclesiastical courts, for their marrying with us, at last have obtained in the civil courts a prohibition until the next term. . . .'[4] The synod advised the persons concerned not to yield to the pressure put upon them to re-marry, and then went on: 'And whereas this interloquitur is informed that this is the case of some, and may be the condition of others, we are resolved, and do firmly purpose, to give our best advice and assistance to any of our people or friends under such circumstances, as also proper support in such cases as may require it'.[5]

Even the overthrow of the high churchmen on the accession of George I did not put an end to these prosecutions, a fact which illustrates the extent to which the ecclesiastical courts were removed from the direct control of the government. Just before the queen's death the Ulster presbyterians had sent a deputation to London to try to obtain redress of their grievances.[6] Though the question of marriages is not actually mentioned in the very general record of their instructions which survives, there can be little doubt that it was one of the grievances intended; for the synod which sent these delegates was the same as that mentioned above which took such a strong line in defence of those who were being prosecuted for marrying in the presbyterian way. In the following year this delegation was able to report that it had been favourably received; but though it held out hopes of redress in other directions, no mention is made of the marriage question.[7]

By 1716 the synod of Ulster was once more petitioning for relief on

---

[1] *Constitutions and canons ecclesiastical* (Dublin, 1714), p. 8.

[2] *Wodrow correspondence*, i. 484 note.

[3] Francis Iredell to the earl of Oxford, 23 Sep. 1713 (*Portland MSS*, v. 340).

[4] *Rec. gen. syn.*, i. 339.   [5] Ibid., i. 339.

[6] Ibid., i. 341.   [7] Ibid., i. 364 ff.

this point. It was decided 'that our brethren in Dublin be desired to apply to the government and lord chancellor, for relief of several persons excommunicated for their marriages . . .'. There follows a list of seven names. But this list is probably incomplete. It includes only one name from the parish of Tullylish; but in the same year the presbyterian minister of the parish wrote to Wodrow, 'Our prelates are violent where I live. Four of my flock have been lately delivered to Satan for being married by me'. Excommunication, which is clearly meant here, would almost certainly involve imprisonment.[1]

There is no evidence of the result of this move; but within a short time the clergy seem to have become alarmed at the hostile public opinion aroused by their policy. In 1718 Archbishop King advised Bishop Smith of Down that in his inquiries into marriages without licences he should include Roman catholics as well as protestant dissenters; any other course would seem, 'especially in your country, a little odious'.[2] This, however, does not seem to have meant any relief for the presbyterians, nor did the toleration act of 1719 improve their position in this respect. The synod of 1722 decided to 'draw a representation of our grievances in the prosecution of our people on account of their being married by our ministers and other particulars, and to draw a petition thereon to the government'.[3] It was probably as a result of this petition that an attempt was made to settle the business by parliamentary action in 1723. The heads of a bill for this purpose were brought into the Irish commons towards the end of 1723,[4] and the lord lieutenant, Grafton, was urged by the presbyterian members to ensure its passage on return from England by tacking it to a measure for the renewal of temporary laws, which was sure to pass.[5] The Irish privy council, however, forwarded the draft to England as a separate bill, and in such a form as would make clandestine marriages very easy. In this form it came back and was rejected by the commons.[6] In the account of the matter sent to Wodrow, Archbishop Synge of Tuam is accused of carrying through this manoeuvre in order to secure the rejection of the bill.[7] There is nothing in Grafton's letters to bear this out; but if the accusa-

[1] Ibid., i. 412, Gilbert Kennedy to Wodrow, 1716 (Wodrow's MS letters, xx, no. 124, quoted in J. Stevenson, *Two centuries of life in Down*, p. 163).
[2] Abp King to Bp Smith of Down, 5 July 1718 (King corr. T.C.D. transcript).
[3] *Rec. gen. syn.*, ii. 38.
[4] Grafton to Carteret, 15 Nov. 1723 (T.S.P.I., T.580, pp. 85–6).
[5] Grafton to ——, 14 Dec. 1723 (ibid., pp. 94–5).
[6] Grafton to Carteret, 12 Feb. 1724 (ibid., p. 113).
[7] Wodrow's MS letters, xxi, no. 86, quoted in Reid, *History*, iii. 221.

tion is true it is a significant indication of the power of the church party in the Irish privy council that it should be able to hold up a measure which the government and the house of commons were united in wishing to pass.

Though foiled in their effort to secure legal protection, the presbyterians seem to have suffered less from prosecutions in the years following this failure.[1] When the government's anxiety about the increase of emigration led to an inquiry into their grievances about 1728, the inconvenience which they suffered on account of their marriages was not urged with any great vigour. When it was mentioned in one of their memorials, Primate Boulter's reply was 'that for some time they had not been molested about their marriages'.[2] But perhaps the clearest evidence of the decline of these prosecutions is to be found in the quietness with which a relief act was eventually passed in 1737. It was passed along with the customary indemnity act, and seems to have aroused neither the gratitude of the presbyterians nor the hostility of their enemies. Its provisions were simple: presbyterian marriages were to be legal and no prosecutions were to arise from them, provided the persons so married and the officiating minister 'have taken or shall take' the oaths in the toleration act of 1719.[3]

This privilege was confirmed by a more explicit declaration and at the same time extended to other protestant dissenters by an act of 1782, which declared that marriages between protestant dissenters performed by a protestant dissenting minister were as good in law as those of the established church.[4] Even then, in spite of the growing feeling of tolerance, the measure met with strenuous opposition in the house of lords. This act left the protestant dissenters only one important ground of complaint in respect of marriages: it was still open to question whether or not a protestant dissenting minister could legally marry two people one of whom was *not* a protestant dissenter. This grievance, which might have seemed trifling in the reign of Anne, survived to cause great bitterness in that of Victoria, until its settlement in 1844.[5]

Lack of material makes it impossible to do more than trace thus in bare outline the history of the agitation conducted by the presbyterians

---

[1] At the synod of 1723 reference was made to presbyterians prosecuted 'for non-conformity'. This probably refers to prosecutions for marriages as well as for such offences as non-payment of tithes. See *Rec. gen. syn.*, ii. 66.

[2] Abp Boulter to Bp Gibson of London, 13 Mar. 1729 (*Boulter letters*, i. 289).

[3] 11 Geo. II c. 10 (Ireland).

[4] 21 & 22 Geo. III, c. 25 (Ireland).

[5] 7 & 8 Vic. c. 81.

for the legalisation of their marriages. No records of ecclesiastical courts survive to show how many people were prosecuted, how many complied with the orders of the court, how many were imprisoned, or for how long. But even the meagre information available, when assembled, serves to illustrate one important truth. The sufferings of the Irish presbyterians in the eighteenth century arose, not from the deliberate policy of the government, but rather from the government's inability to give them effective protection when the law provided their enemies, the high churchmen, with any weapon against them. This fact, which has already been commented on in the account given above of the abjuration oath,[1] is seen once more in this history of the marriage question.

[1] Ch. VI.

XII

THE MINOR SECTS

The position of the Irish presbyterians in the eighteenth century cannot be fully understood unless some account is given of the other protestant dissenters. The means of comparison thus provided will fix more clearly the motives behind the hostility so often shown to the presbyterians and to all proposals to improve their status. It will not be necessary to trace in detail the history of the various bodies of protestant dissenters, but merely to indicate the points at which the more important of them came into contact with the government and the treatment they received. From this survey we may exclude those various bodies of presbyterians which were not connected with the synod of Ulster but held the same political position.

A beginning may be made with the French protestants whose doctrine and discipline approximated very closely to those of the presbyterians. The legal position which they were to occupy during the eighteenth century and indeed until their final absorption into the rest of the population, was settled in the reign of William III. Though French protestants had come to Ireland during the reigns of Charles II and James II[1] it was not until after the revolution that the great influx began. The early settlers had been largely concentrated in Dublin, and there the Lady chapel of St. Patrick's cathedral was provided for their worship on condition that they conformed to the church of Ireland.[2] When the position of the French protestants was reconsidered at the beginning of William III's reign the circumstances were different. The settlers were more numerous; they were scattered in separate groups over the kingdom; the outlook of the government was more tolerant. In December 1690 the king ordered the lords justices to 'propose some way of settlement for the French church in Ireland, and in the meantime to take care of M. Roussel the French minister'.[3] This Roussel (or Rossel) was minister of the conforming congregation in St. Patrick's.[4] So far no

---

[1] The general history of these earlier settlers is summarized in A. Carré, *L'influence des huguenots français en Irelande aux xviie et xviiie siècles* (Paris, 1937), pp. 2–9. More detailed accounts of the various settlements are in G. L. Lee, *The huguenot settlements in Ireland* (London, 1936).

[2] Carré, op. cit., p. 114; Lee, op. cit., p. 219.

[3] Nottingham to the lords justices of Ireland, 2 Dec. 1690 (*Cal. S. P. dom., 1690–1*, p. 176).

[4] Lee, op. cit., p. 230.

regular system for his maintenance had been arranged, for early in 1692 he was paid £25 'as of his majesty's bounty for his present support until he shall be established'.[1] Apparently his establishment soon took place for there is no record of petition for payments, such as came from other French congregations.

The early settlers had been too poor and too helpless to resist the pressure put on them to conform to the established church.[2] But now came a demand that they should be allowed to organise their worship and discipline after their own fashion. The matter was considered during 1692. In July of that year the earl of Galway proposed that those congregations which wished to follow the order of the reformed churches of France might do so, provided they obtained letters patent of the king for each place in which they settled. This proposal is endorsed 'offered and read to council; rejected'.[3] But in the same year an act was passed which gave all that Galway seemed to ask. This laid down that all protestant strangers, having taken certain oaths, etc. 'shall have and enjoy the free exercise of their religion, and have liberty of meeting together publicly for the worship of God and of hearing divine service, and performing other religious duties in their own several rites used in their own countries; any law or statute to the contrary notwithstanding'.[4] When the rejection of Galway's proposal is considered along with the terms of this act, it seems probable that what he really meant was that congregations of French protestants in receipt of royal grants might be free to conform or not as they chose. If this is so, then the government in rejecting his suggestion did not intend to limit religious freedom but merely to ensure that those ministers who were supported by the state conformed to the state church.

Meanwhile the number of immigrants was increasing, and the importance attached by the government to this influx is seen from the proposals to bring protestants not only directly from France but also from Switzerland, whither many of them had fled;[5] memoranda on this project were drawn up for the English government in February and December 1692.[6] Early in 1693 correspondence on the subject passed

---

[1] Payment and receipt book, revenue and army, Ireland, June 1690–March 1691 (P.R.O.N.I., T.689, p. 95).

[2] Carré, op. cit., pp. 114–5.

[3] Cal. S. P. dom., Wm III (addenda), p. 193.

[4] 4 Wm & Mary c. 2 (Ireland).

[5] Carré, op. cit., pp. 11–12.

[6] Cal. S. P. dom., 1691–2, pp. 138, 453; instructions to lords lieutenant to encourage protestant strangers had been common form since the reign of Charles II.

between the lord lieutenant and Nottingham,[1] but in the following year the scheme broke down for lack of money.[2] Another and very different indication of the growing importance of the huguenots is to be seen in the jealousy aroused by the numerous positions which they occupied in the army, to the exclusion, it was said, of Irish protestants who had fought for William in the revolutionary wars.[3] It was partly to allay this jealousy that the king ordered the disbandment of many of the French regiments in Ireland in the following year (1699).[4] A more generous spirit is seen in the proposal made and executed in 1701 that the money collected for the persecuted Vaudois and no longer needed for that purpose should be applied to the relief of needy French protestant refugees.[5] But by far the most outstanding recognition of the national importance of the huguenot immigration was that given by the Irish house of commons. In 1695 they received two petitions from the French protestants asking for various privileges and for provision for their ministers.[6] Immediately on receipt of the second petition the commons set up a committee, which reported favourably.[7] The house thereupon drew up a petition of its own on behalf of the French protestants and presented it to the lord deputy (10 December 1695). This dealt explicitly with the question of religion: 'that they who have been forced to leave their native country on account of their religion may not want that for which they have fled hither, we presume to recommend most earnestly to your excellency's consideration the providing for a competent number of orthodox ministers, who conform to the liturgy of the church of England, by allowing them such salaries as his majesty shall think fit to put on the establishment of this kingdom'.[8] The commons, it seems, were determined not to endow any dissenters. French protestants as useful citizens were to be given every encouragement to settle; but unless they conformed they were to expect no assistance for their religion beyond a mere toleration.

The non-conformists, however, realising that they would probably get more from the English government than from the Irish parliament, sent, in the next year, a memorial to the king, through Lord Capel. From this it appears that there were six non-conforming congregations

[1] *Cal. S. P. dom., 1693*, pp. 33, 50, 90.

[2] Irish privy council to ——, 5 Mar. 1694; Charles de Sailly to Lord ——, 6 Mar. 1694 (*Cal. S. P. dom., 1694–5*, pp. 51, 53).

[3] *Cal. S. P. dom., 1698*, pp. 397–8.

[4] *Cal. S. P. dom., 1699–1700*, pp. 101, 105.

[5] *Cal. S. P. dom., 1700–2*, pp. 223, 285, 310.

[6] *Commons' jn. Ire.*, ii. 529, 600.

[7] Ibid., ii. 600, 604–5.   [8] Ibid., ii. 628.

and that the king had promised each of them a grant for the support of a minister.[1] This memorial was sent to England at the same time as the petition of the house of commons on behalf of the conforming congregations.[2] Capel backed up the plea for help for non-conforming ministers,[3] but though the king acknowledged the receipt of both petitions he gave no immediate reply to either,[4] and the further result does not appear. It would seem that some provision was made for non-conforming as well as for conforming French protestants; for in 1702 Bishop Lindsay of Killaloe, who was in London at the time, petitioned unsuccessfully against a bill in the English parliament relating to church endowments in Portarlington, on the ground that it placed the non-conforming and conforming congregations on an equality.[5]

In the increased hostility manifested against protestant dissenters in the reign of Anne the non-conforming French protestants did not entirely escape attention, though they seem to have suffered little. Archbishop King complained that the French congregation at Carlow had received as minister one who had been ordained by 'schismatical presbyters among ourselves' and expressed the fear that if they continued in this way 'they will place themselves on the same foot with the dissenters in relation to church communion, which would be of ill consequence both to them and us'.[6] The author of the *Conduct of the dissenters* declared that the toleration given to other protestant dissenters (i.e. presbyterians) had encouraged some French protestants who had conformed to the established church to break away.[7] If this is true it indicates that such conformity was not always whole-hearted. But there is no other evidence of such relapses into non-conformity, and the majority of the French protestants seem to have accepted the forms of the established church without serious reluctance. Those who did not were left in peace; sympathy for their sufferings, a due appreciation of their value to the community, and the smallness of their numbers[8] all

---

[1] The congregations were Dublin (two ministers), Cork, Waterford, Carlow, Portarlington, Castleblayney (*Cal. S. P. dom., 1696*, p. 6).

[2] Ibid., p. 5.

[3] Capel to Shrewsbury, 3 Jan. 1696 (ibid., p. 5).

[4] Shrewsbury to Capel, 21 Jan. 1696 (ibid., p. 23).

[5] Petition of Thomas, lord bishop of Killaloe against a bill for the relief of Francis Spring and others with relation to the forfeited estates in Ireland, 22 May 1702 (*House of lords MSS*, new series, v. 49–50).

[6] Abp King to Bp Vigors of Ferns, ?1710 (King corr. T.C.D., transcript).

[7] *Conduct of the dissenters* (Dublin, 1712), p. 17.

[8] Carré estimates the huguenots at the height of the immigration at about 10,000 (op. cit., p. 112).

contributing to ensure their toleration. This toleration, established in King William's reign, was never disturbed. The act of 1692 was continued by 2 Anne c. 14 and made perpetual by 4 George I c. 9. An incident in the adventurous life of James Fontaine illustrates the degree of toleration extended to the huguenots. In 1698 he was minister of a non-conforming congregation in Cork. A section of his congregation, wishing to get rid of him, complained to the bishop who complained to Lord Galway that he had not received episcopal ordination. But though Fontaine resigned it was rather to avoid a split in his congregation than under government pressure. Not only was he able to secure the appointment of a successor of the same religious principles as himself, but he continued to preach regularly in a presbyterian church in Cork without any interference.[1] Thus easily did the French protestants secure the legal toleration for which the presbyterians so long struggled in vain. Nor is that the only striking contrast: the presbyterians to whom legal toleration was denied steadily refused to conform, while among the French protestants to whom it was so freely extended comparatively few took advantage of it.

From first to last then, the French protestants in Ireland were treated by the government with special consideration; conformity was made profitable and non-conformity easy. Even during the period of high church domination, in 1711, a second non-conforming congregation was established in Dublin.[2] Some of the grounds on which this tolerant policy was no doubt based have already been suggested; another remains. The huguenots were regarded not merely as refugees to be helped, but also as valuable contributors to the national wealth. The importance of their influence in Ireland during this period has been described and assessed by Dr Carré.[3] Here it is enough to note that the huguenots insisted and the government realised that since the main purpose of their coming to Ireland had been to secure religious freedom, this freedom must be granted if they were to be useful members of the community.[4] In Louis Crommelin's petition of 1699, setting out his plan for establishing the linen industry of Ireland on a firm basis by the labour of French protestants he suggests the need for providing French ministers paid by the government wherever there is a French colony.[5] Again, when

[1] *Memoirs of a huguenot family translated and compiled from the original autobiography of the Reverend James Fontaine*, pp. 169–72, 176.

[2] Carré, op. cit., p. 116.

[3] Op. cit.

[4] Cf. petition of the houses of commons in 1695 and Capel's support of the non-conforming huguenots in 1696 (above, pp. 126–7).

[5] P.R.O., Treasury papers, in Carré, op. cit., pp. 136–7.

the huguenot colony at Kilkenny petitioned for a minister 'established upon the civil list of this kingdom, with such salary as your majesty in your great wisdom shall think sufficient', they gave as one reason for granting their request that it would encourage the linen manufacture.[1]

A logical government would have perceived that what applied to the French protestants applied no less to the presbyterians, and that the skill and industry of the latter, from their immensely greater numbers, would be even more important in developing the wealth of the country; that therefore prudence, if not justice or humanity, would secure to them an equal degree of religious freedom. That the Irish government refused to see the situation in this light is further proof that their policy towards the presbyterians was based less on reason than on prejudice and on jealousy. Yet it may be claimed, at the risk of a paradox, that the prejudice and the jealousy were not in themselves unreasonable; for in their disputes with the church the presbyterians assumed a tone of superiority more commonly than one of supplication, and in their organisation they seemed to encroach upon the established powers both ecclesiastical and civil. Besides this, whereas the increasing wealth of the huguenots was a manifest gain to the whole community, their numbers being so small that though they might make wealth for themselves they could not keep it to themselves, the increasing wealth of the presbyterians seemed to the churchmen a threat to their own position. One of their bitterest complaints was that the protestant dissenters of Ulster deliberately kept trade in the hands of their own community. It was trade, so Bishop King was assured by one of his flock in Londonderry, which had given the presbyterians 'means and power to oppose and injure us and has procured them an interest and friends to assist them in their unjust designs'.[2] Twelve years later the author of the *Conduct of the dissenters* was complaining that the linen trade was almost completely in the hands of the presbyterians.[3] In 1711 the Irish house of lords in their address to the queen on the state of religion included in their complaints against the presbyterians the charge that they attempted to monopolize trade in their own hands.[4] It is not then altogether surprising to find that while the wealth of the huguenots was looked upon as a national asset that of the presbyterians was regarded with suspicion and apprehension, and as an additional motive for keeping from them the opportunity to employ it in politics.

[1] 'Ireland: clergy and church affairs (1568–1725)' (B.M. Add. MS, 21, 132), in Carré, op. cit., p. 139.

[2] Charles Norman to Bp King, 1 Jan. 1699 (King corr. T.C.D.).

[3] *Conduct of the dissenters*, p. 17.

[4] *Lords' jn. Ire.*, ii. 410–11.

As early as 1691 it had been suggested that colonies of German as well as of French protestants should be established in Ireland.[1] But though some sort of start seems to have been made in the following year with protestants from Silesia,[2] and though the directions given to successive lord lieutenants ordered them to encourage all protestant strangers,[3] no extensive settlement of German protestants was attempted until towards the end of Queen Anne's reign. Then, however, the desolation of the Palatinate suggested to the English government the humanity of offering an asylum to the distressed inhabitants, and the hope of strengthening the Irish protestant interest indicated the suitability of providing that asylum in Ireland. In October 1709, accordingly, a commission including the lords justices, the archbishops of Armagh and Dublin, the bishops of Kildare and Clogher and a considerable number of noblemen and gentlemen was appointed to supervise the settlement of the palatines in Ireland.[4] The fullest contemporary account of the number and condition of the new settlers is to be found in the report presented by this commission eighteen months later.[5] From this it appears that rather over three thousand palatines arrived, but that when the report was made only about two thousand, comprising five hundred and seven families, remained in Ireland. The rest, apart from those who had died, had returned to England. They were almost entirely dependent upon government provision, and though brought over to settle on the land the majority of them were in Dublin.

Up to this point there is no indication that the government had made any provision for the spiritual welfare of these protestant strangers. Unlike the huguenots, they do not seem to have brought any ministers with them, nor was any building provided for their religious services. When eventually a considerable number of them were settled on different estates in various parts of the kingdom they conformed, apparently without complaint, to the established church. In 1712 Archbishop King wrote from Killbrae, 'All the palatines conform to the church but are at a loss for a minister; they have a common prayer book in German and English with which they are much pleased'.[6] Three years later the lords justices give the same evidence in a report to the lord lieutenant,

[1] 'Considerations concerning Ireland', in *Cal. S. P. dom., 1691–2*, p. 67.
[2] Sydney to ——, 8 Oct. 1692 (*Cal. S. P. dom., Wm III (addenda)*, p. 211).
[3] See above, p. 125.
[4] Palatine papers (Queen's letters, carton 160, no. 337).
[5] Palatine papers (Queen's entry book of letters and reports, vol. 15, I.E. 2. 6, pp. 55–7).
[6] Abp King to Southwell, 26 Mar. 1712 (King corr. T.C.D., N. 3. 4, pt. 1, p. 22).

'They are become members of our church, and constant communicants therewith'.[1]

The palatines, then, cannot be classed as dissenters. Circumstances and not persecution compelled them to conform. They were too poor and too few to receive the same consideration as the non-conforming French protestants; nor do any of their petitions suggest that they were dissatisfied with their treatment in the matter of religion. Even when in 1712 they tried to get permission and help to leave Ireland, and having no minister of their own enlisted the support of the minister of the Prussian church in the Savoy, it was of temporal and not spiritual wants that they complained.[2]

Of what may be called the native protestant sects by far the most important, apart from the presbyterians, was the society of friends or quakers. Even during the reign of James II, when other protestants had either left the kingdom or found their lives and property in danger, the quakers received special consideration. On one occasion, for instance, they complained to Tyrconnell of ill-treatment at the hands of Roman catholic soldiers. The case was investigated, the delinquents punished and the company removed from the neighbourhood.[3] Their influence even extended to securing protection for other protestants, and the favour shown by James II to Penn was shared by his Irish co-religionists.[4] Of the period of that king's sojourn in Ireland, William Edmundson writes: 'In those times I was much at Dublin, applying to the government on behalf of the country, for the Lord had given friends favour with the government and they would hear my complaint. . . . I was sometimes with King James, and told him of the calamity the protestants were under in the country, and he would hear me quietly, for the Lord made way in their hearts for us'.[5] James on his side found the quakers useful. When he came into Ireland he caused a bleaching and weaving establishment to be handed over to 'one Bromfield, a quaker, to furnish his army'.[6]

It might have been expected that other Irish protestants would have felt some resentment at this favourable treatment of quakers; and in particular at the fact that while other protestants were being deprived of

[1] Palatine papers .(King's entry book of letters and reports, vol. 20, I.E. 2. 11, pp. 273–6).

[2] J. J. Caesar to [John Chamberlayne?], 16 June 1712 (*Portland MSS*, v. 183–4).

[3] W. Edmundson, *Journal* (Dublin, 1715), p. 114.

[4] King, *State of the protestants of Ireland*, pp. 203–4.

[5] Edmundson, *Journal*, p. 120.

[6] *Cal. S. P. dom., 1690–1*, p. 338.

magistracies and of positions on corporations, such offices were offered to quakers and apparently accepted by them.[1] Had any such resentment existed it would have appeared after the revolution. But from the first the government of William III showed every disposition to treat the quakers well, especially in the matter of oaths, where they were most likely to suffer for their non-conformity to the usual practice of the times. In the act of 1691 which abrogated the oath of supremacy in Ireland and appointed other oaths, a special form of declaration to be made by quakers was inserted.[2] Neither in England nor in Ireland, however, were quakers exempt from taking the usual oaths in law-courts and their failure to do so was a frequent cause of loss to them. In 1692 a bill was introduced into the English parliament to enable them to make affirmations instead. The Irish quakers communicated with their brethren in London on the subject but without immediate result.[3]

But though they suffered pecuniary loss on this account the greatest danger arose from their refusal to pay tithes. It was principally for this reason that they suffered imprisonment, though on their own computation the total number imprisoned during the reign of William III was only thirty-three.[4] Moreover, these imprisonments probably took place at intervals over the whole reign, for at the 'third month national meeting' in 1695, it was considered worth while observing 'that no one friend was a prisoner throughout the nation, friends having gained a pretty good esteem among those in authority'.[5] This esteem extended to members of parliament. For in the same year the commons passed the heads of a bill to relieve quakers from dangers to which they might be exposed from the terms of one of the popery acts.[6] In this year also the quakers were able to enlist the support of members of both houses in opposition to a tithe bill;[7] and an address was favourably received.[8] Another attempt, in 1697, to pass a bill empowering magistrates to imprison for non-payment of tithes was resisted by similar means.[9] The English government agreed that this part of the bill was too severe and

---

[1] T. Wight & J. Rutty, *History of the quakers in Ireland* (London, 1811), pp. 142–3.

[2] 3 Wm & Mary c. 2 (England).

[3] Wight & Rutty, op. cit., p. 161.

[4] Ibid., p. 325.

[5] Ibid., p. 163.

[6] *Commons' jn. Ire.*, ii. 611, 613, 635.

[7] Edmundson, *Journal*, p. 149.

[8] Ibid., p. 151.

[9] Ibid., p. 172; Vernon to Williamson, 3 Aug. 1697 (*Cal. S. P. dom., 1697* p. 280).

it was omitted.[1] But parliament was not always so favourable, and in 1697 the lords rejected two bills because of clauses exempting quakers from the necessity of taking oaths.[2]

Meanwhile, however, the quakers seem to have held their meetings freely throughout the country. Occasionally their zeal brought them into conflict with clergy or magistrates, and not infrequently they came off best. Time after time during the reigns of William and Anne, Edmundson recounts how he held meetings in spite of strong opposition.[3] On one occasion when he and his friends were put in the stocks for their preaching the disapproval shown by the crowd 'some of whom wept to see an ancient man set in the stocks for worshipping God, having never seen the like before' was so marked that they were speedily released.[4] In fact, those magistrates who tried to take a strong line against the quakers generally found themselves in such an uncomfortable position between fear of the government and fear of the powerful supporters whom the quakers seemed to find everywhere in the kingdom that they were usually glad enough to set them at liberty again.[5] Even during the reign of Queen Anne they suffered less than the presbyterians from the prevalent high church feeling.

But while they thus enjoyed immunity from persecution merely for their non-conformity, the quakers had so far received no general redress of their three main grievances—oaths, tithes, the militia. The last of these was first to be settled. In 1715 an act of the Irish parliament for the regulation of the militia provided special treatment for quakers.[6] Their grievance on this head was the opposite of that of the presbyterians: not that they were excluded from commissions, but that they were liable to suffer for their conscientious refusal either to bear arms or to take the oaths imposed on those who wished to secure exemption. This act allowed them to compound for personal service on the same terms as other protestants upon making an affirmation of their loyalty to the king and denying the claims of the pope and the pretender. It was perhaps to this that Archbishop King referred when he wrote in the following year to the archbishop of Canterbury expressing his satisfaction that the Irish quakers had at last been put on the same standing as

---

[1] Shrewsbury to the lords justices of Ireland, 3 Aug. 1697 (*Buccleuch and Queensbury MSS*, ii, (pt. ii), 516); same to same, 12 Aug. 1697 (ibid., p. 530).

[2] Methuen to Shrewsbury, 27 Nov. 1697 (ibid., p. 584). News letter, 7 Dec. 1697, in *Cal. S. P. dom., 1697*, p. 502.

[3] Edmundson, *Journal*, pp. 179–180, 181, 189–90, 249–50.

[4] Ibid., pp. 188–9.

[5] E.g. at Kilkenny in 1717 (Wight & Rutty, op. cit., pp. 220 ff.).

[6] 2 Geo. I c. 9.

those of England.[1] In 1723 they were given a temporary indulgence in the matter of oaths.[2] This act was to remain in force for three years. It was renewed, with some alterations, in 1727 for seven years, in 1735 for eleven years, and made perpetual in 1745.[3] But no quaker was to hold any post of profit under the crown by virtue of this indulgence, though not excluded from the freedom of cities and towns.

In the meantime quakers, like other protestant dissenters, had had their practical toleration confirmed to them by the act of 1719. The only grievance which remained was that of tithes. This indeed was a grievance which was shared by the rest of the population, and not only by the dissenters; but with the quakers it was a matter not of money but of conscience. In 1740 a sort of questionnaire was issued to their monthly and quarterly meetings, of which the fourteenth point was, 'Do friends maintain their testimony against paying or receiving tithes, church rates, and all kinds of priests' dues so called?'[4] The treatment which they received for non-payment of tithes varied considerably from place to place and from time to time. It depended almost entirely upon the temper of those with whom they had to deal. The government was able to prevent the passing of repressive acts enforcing payment, but could not or would not interfere with the carrying out of the existing law. In 1691 Bishop King advocated extreme measures: 'My opinion is that you ought to send your servants, or if they resist them, the militia, and bring away your tithes. 'Tis the only method takes with them . . .'[5] A few years later Edmundson tells how he interviewed a clergyman who had cited some quakers before the bishop's court for non-payment of tithes, and found him very friendly and reasonable.[6] In 1711 the quakers were still trying to secure government support to mitigate their hardships on this account,[7] but, although by this time they had the support of at least one bishop,[8] without much success. Nevertheless, though they still suffered loss in money and property, imprisonments became rarer. By the middle of the eighteenth century their position was secure.

[1] Abp King to Abp Wake of Canterbury, 8 May 1716 (King corr. T.C.D., transcript).

[2] 10 Geo. I c. 8. The indulgence granted by this act extended to most cases connected with trade, to the obtaining of freedoms in cities and boroughs, and to the recovery of rent where title to land was not in question.

[3] 1 Geo. II c. 5; 9 Geo. II c. 16; 19 Geo. II c. 18.

[4] Wight & Rutty, op. cit., p. 304.

[5] Bp King to Foley, 31 July 1691 (King corr. T.C.D.).

[6] Edmundson, *Journal*, pp. 145–6.

[7] Abp King to Swift, 27 Oct. 1711 (Mant, *Ch. of Ire.*, p. 227).

[8] Bp Ashe of Clogher (Pearson to earl of Oxford, 24 June 1711, *Portland MSS*, v. 22).

As they themselves admitted, 'The chief sufferings of friends are for tithes, priests' maintenance, and other ecclesiastical demands, and during these twenty-one years, there have been but six prisoners on this account'.[1]

The history of the quakers follows fairly closely that of the presbyterians. Though, like the huguenots, they did receive some special legislative provision before the general toleration of 1719, this was only in respect of those peculiar doctrines and practices which could be indulged without any interference with the rights or privileges of others. And even here the opposition to the government's policy, especially in the matter of oaths, was strong enough to procure its modification. Where the conscience of the quakers threatened the interest of the church, as in their refusal to pay tithes, all that they could secure was a check on attempts to make the law more rigorous. It is worth noting, however, that while the opposition to the presbyterians was on many occasions strong in the house of commons, the opposition to the quakers was always found in the house of lords, where clerical influence was more powerful. The motives which caused the landlords to fear the presbyterians could not move them against the quakers, so that they were willing to treat the latter more leniently than the lords who, whether from principle or from prejudice, were more consistent in their opposition to toleration.

The quakers occupy a position midway between the presbyterians and the huguenots. Like the latter they were small in numbers, wealthy themselves and a source of wealth to the country; but they had no special claim on the compassion of the people or the government, and like the presbyterians they were often outspoken in their opposition to the established church. This midway position is reflected in their treatment. They did not receive the speedy and complete toleration which was accorded to the non-conforming French protestants, but the government succeeded in securing special relief for them before it was able to secure any similar legislation in favour of the presbyterians. The general conclusion is obvious. The Irish parliament was induced to acquiesce in religious toleration not on grounds of principle but on grounds of expediency. To the French protestants, distressed and helpless, it was granted at once; to the quakers, not numerous but suspected both for their principles and their conduct, by degrees; to the presbyterians, dangerous by their numbers, hated for the past and feared for the future, only under the strongest pressure.

Of the other groups of protestant dissenters there is little to say.

[1] Wight & Rutty, op. cit., p. 328. The 21 years are 1727–48. The last prisoner was confined for a short time in 1743 (ibid., p. 326).

Considered numerically they were of no importance; and unlike the huguenots and quakers they did not derive importance from any other circumstance. Accurate statistics of the distribution of religious denominations in Ireland in the eighteenth century do not exist; but some idea of the size of the smaller sects may be gained from the number of congregations which each possessed in the early nineteenth century. In 1836 there were twenty-eight congregations of independents, sixteen of baptists and seven of moravians.[1] But none of these bodies can trace a connected history throughout the eighteenth century, though certain independent congregations in Dublin seem to be directly descended from those formed by ministers who were expelled from their livings in the reign of Charles II.[2] Eighteenth-century Ireland was not favourable to the subdivision of sects, and both independents and baptists, numerous enough under the commonwealth, survived into modern times only by reason of missionary effort on the part of the stronger communities in England.[3] The first moravian congregation was established in Ireland about 1757, as a result of a split among the followers of Whitefield, who visited the country in that year.[4] But though they engaged in missionary activities, and exerted some influence on the religious life of the country, they never became numerous and never attracted the attention of the government.

Like the moravians, the methodists did not appear in Ireland until half way through the eighteenth century; but properly speaking they do not fall within the scope of this work, for during the period under review they remained, theoretically at least, members of the established church. The early history of methodism in Ireland does show one thing, however. It makes it quite plain that the act of uniformity, even as it existed after 1719, could no longer be enforced. When John Wesley first visited Ireland in 1747 he was informed, first by a friend, then by the archbishop of Dublin himself, that lay preaching and preaching out of church would not be tolerated.[5] In spite of this Wesley's journal makes it abundantly clear that meetings were held both indoors and out all over Ireland and addressed by both clergy and laymen. The opposition party among the clergy and landlords found it impossible to achieve anything by legal means, and were obliged to rely on the violence of the mob, which could often be incited against the itinerant preachers and

[1] Mathews, *Account of the regium donum*, p. 64.

[2] Five of the independent congregations were in Dublin city (ibid., p. 64).

[3] *Political Christianity* (London, 1834), pp. 76–8, 81.

[4] *Life and times of Selina, countess of Huntingdon*, ii. 154.

[5] J. Wesley, *Journal*, ed. Curnock, iii. 312–13; C. H. Crookshank, *History of methodism in Ireland*, i. 16.

their hearers. On one occasion in Cork, it is true, the sequel to such riots was a presentation by the grand jury against Charles Wesley and others; but the English government, moved by Lady Huntingdon, speedily showed its displeasure.[1] But in general the methodists had little contact with the government. Their society was organised within the established church as a complementary, not a rival institution. The very existence of the society and its manner of working proved both the spiritual weakness of the established church and its inability to enforce discipline. With the former of these the state was little concerned; and it showed no disposition to assist in remedying the latter.

The political significance which in Ireland has usually attached to religious divisions tended during the eighteenth century to obliterate all distinctions save that of protestant and papist. To establish and maintain this distinction as the basis of policy in church and state was one of the main aims of the English government, especially during the first half of the century. In previous chapters it has been shown how the suspicion with which the established church regarded the presbyterians was a constant hindrance to the attaining of this aim. But the tendency was nevertheless present; and if it did not succeed in uniting church and presbytery at least it checked the growth of sects, and by leaving little room for other shades of opinion effected a sort of stabilisation of the religious situation. Even when the presbyterians split among themselves they endeavoured to maintain a united front to the world in all matters of common interest.

Though the quakers maintained a separate existence the other forms which protestantism had assumed during the commonwealth fell back after the restoration to the two broad divisions of presbyterianism and episcopacy. The non-conforming huguenots maintained their distinction rather from national than from religious feeling, and as the former subsided the distinction disappeared. It was only after a long time that the Irish methodists were organised as a separate sect, and even then a considerable section of them (primitive methodists) maintained their connection with the established church.[2] This tendency against subdivision meant that the minor bodies of protestant dissenters were insignificant in numbers when compared to the presbyterians. This in itself was enough to secure for them more tolerant treatment. But this was not the only or the principal reason for their immunity. Unlike the presbyterians their religious position neither had nor was suspected of having any political significance. Presbyterianism, on the other hand, was not only hated as religious dissent, but suspected as a

[1] *Life and times of Selina, countess of Huntingdon*, ii. 150-151.
[2] *Political Christianity*, pp. 83–4.

force inimical to the landlords and even to the state. The prevalence of this suspicion, however unfounded, and the comparative immunity of the other protestant dissenters combine to prove once more from another angle that the high church opposition to toleration and to repeal of the sacramental test was based less on conscientious scruples than on fear of the presbyterians.

XIII

THE ECONOMIC STATUS OF THE PROTESTANT DISSENTERS

'The bulk of the common people of Ireland', wrote Archbishop King in 1715, 'are either papists or dissenters, equally enemies to the established church: but the gentry are generally conformable, and the church interest apparently lies in them'.[1] The substantial truth of this cannot be disputed; for though the Cromwellian settlement had brought in many presbyterian and independent landlords, the vast majority of these had conformed within a short period after the restoration. But some closer examination of the economic and social status of the presbyterians is necessary to a full understanding of their relations with the government during the period under review. There are two questions to be answered. First, what was the connection between the economic status of the presbyterians and their virtual exclusion from any share in the government? Secondly, what means did they possess of countering the effects of this exclusion?

To begin with, something must be said of their influence in parliament. In the house of lords they had none. The bishops were naturally opposed to dissent; the temporal lords were even more intolerant than the commons, and there is no evidence to show that after the exclusion of the Roman catholic peers in the reign of William III there was a single one who was not at least a professing anglican.[2] In the house of commons, however, there was throughout the century a small body of presbyterian members. In 1696 King reckoned their numbers at 'hardly ten'. The significance of this is brought out in his next sentence: 'It has been the business of most of our governors since the revolution to make an interest for dissenters'.[3] There is a good deal of truth in this latter statement, and it is almost certain that there would have been more dissenters in the commons if there had been more of them qualified for election. Twenty years later, when the test was in force, King reported the number of dissenters in the house as only about half-a-dozen; and he clearly says that this represents the extent of their political influence

---

[1] Abp King to Dr Charlett, 20 Apr. 1715 (Mant, *Ch. of Ire.*, p. 293).

[2] In the reign of Charles II, Lord Massereene and Lord Granard had shown themselves very friendly towards the presbyterians; but they had no successors.

[3] Bp King to Bp Lloyd of Lichfield, 15 Dec. 1696 (Mant, *Ch. of Ire.*, p. 69).

in the kingdom.[1] Later still, in 1723, we find Grafton speaking of 'chiefs of the presbyterians in this country who are members of the house of commons';[2] but the phrase is ambiguous, and may have referred merely to politicians who looked for presbyterian support outside parliament. In the northern counties the number of presbyterian voters must certainly have been great; but it is improbable that they often voted against the directions of their landlords. A notable exception to this was the county Antrim election of 1715, when Colonel Upton, a presbyterian and a whig, was returned against the united efforts of the bishop, the clergy and the bulk of the landlords.[3] There was, however, no similar example of independence until 1790, when the popular party in county Down elected Robert Stewart (afterwards Lord Castlereagh) against all the interest of the Hill family. In this great contest the presbyterian vote, organised by William Steel Dickson, presbyterian minister at Portaferry, played a great and probably decisive part.[4] But few presbyterian landlords were wealthy enough to fight a county election and it is probable that most of the presbyterian members were borough representatives. In Londonderry, for example, the presbyterian party in the corporation got rid of a possible church of Ireland candidate for parliament by having him nominated as sheriff; and this would suggest a determination to put in one of their own faith.[5] But direct influence of this sort was brought to an end by the test act, which compelled all members of municipal corporations to conform or resign. Though there was some delay in enforcing this, within a few years the corporations had become the preserve of the established church.[6]

Partly, then, as the indirect result of the sacramental test, partly through their economic circumstances, protestant dissenters were virtually excluded from parliament. Boulter's suggestion, in 1732, that if the dissenters wished to push the repeal of the test 'they should make the best interest they can against another session', implies that they could influence the house of commons only indirectly, by trying to win the support of such members as could be induced to listen to them.[7] But this exclusion was less important than might at first sight appear. The life of the community was much more closely affected by local than by

---

[1] Abp King to Bp Ashe of Clogher, 8 Feb. 1716 (King corr. T.C.D., transcript).

[2] Grafton to ——, 14 Dec. 1723 (T.S.P.I., T.580, pp. 94–5).

[3] *Conduct of the dissenters*, p. 48; Reid, *History*, iii. 70–1.

[4] Stevenson, *Two centuries of life in Down*, pp. 279–80.

[5] Dean Bolton to Bp King, 4 Oct. 1702 (King corr., T.C.D.).

[6] See above, pp. 48–9.

[7] Abp to Newcastle, 15 Jan. 1732 (T.S.P.I., T.722, pp. 10 ff.).

central government: the corporations in the towns, the grand juries and justices of the peace in the counties, often had more influence on the everyday life of the people than parliament had. It was probably their exclusion from these bodies, and especially from the municipal corporations, which gave the protestant dissenters their most solid ground of complaint.

The grand jury consisted of the important landowners of the county and few, if any, presbyterians would qualify for membership. Grand juries, indeed, were outstandingly hostile to toleration; it was the grand jury of Monaghan which presented an entire presbytery for unlawful and riotous assembly at Belturbet in 1712 and the grand jury of Cork took similar action against Charles Wesley and his colleagues in 1749.[1] In the regular and local administration of the law, however, the justices of the peace were of greater importance than the grand juries, and the test act was so interpreted as to make protestant dissenters ineligible for appointment. How many might have been appointed if no restriction had existed is not clear. Some magistrates certainly resigned rather than take the test, but contemporary writers seem to have estimated the number who did so according to their own political outlook. Reid's statement that 'most of the magistrates throughout Ulster were . . . deprived of their commissions' is not supported by the evidence he brings forward, which merely shows that very few *presbyterian* magistrates conformed in order to preserve their posts, but does not provide any reliable statistics of the numbers involved. Whatever may have been the position in 1704, Boulter's opinion, less than thirty years later, was that in the whole province of Ulster there were not a score of protestant dissenters of sufficient property to be made magistrates.[2] Boulter was favourably disposed towards the dissenters and had no reason for putting forward a false estimate nor was he likely to be deceived in such a matter.

The application of the test act to municipal corporations was a much sorer blow to presbyterian power. It had, of course, an effect upon parliamentary representation. In many borough constituencies (Belfast, for example) members of parliament were elected by the corporations; though the influence of a local landlord was often so strong that the election was a mere matter of confirming the appointment of his nominees. In matters of local government, however, the power of the corporation was real and the enforced change was correspondingly resented.[3]

[1] See above, pp. 55, 137.
[2] Reid, *History*, ii. 512; Abp Boulter to Newcastle, 15 Jan. 1732 (T.S.P.I., T.722, p. 13); and see above, pp. 86–7.
Benn, *History of Belfast* (ed. 1877), pp. 565 ff.

It is not to be supposed that the presbyterians, conscious of their numerical strength, were prepared to give up all claims to power. Their closely-knit ecclesiastical organisation enabled them to exercise a real authority outside and even contrary to the civil law. The power of the kirk-sessions was very considerable, especially where presbyterians formed the bulk of the population, and this naturally aroused the jealousy not only of the clergy but also of the landlords. This ecclesiastical jurisdiction was exercised over a wide variety of crimes: fornication, slander, scolding, domestic quarrelling, 'neglect of gospel ordinances', 'profanation of the sabbath', witchcraft. The authority of the kirk-session seems to have been generally accepted among presbyterians, partly, perhaps, owing to the force of tradition, but partly also because the session's power of excommunication carried with it consequences similar to those of a modern boycott.[1] In Belfast, presbyterian influence was so strong that for a time the same sort of moral supervision was carried on, under their pressure, by the constables with the authority of the sovereign.[2]

The ability of the presbyterians to maintain this strong hold on authority depended partly on their numbers, partly on their close organisation, partly on their wealth. In total population the presbyterians probably equalled the members of the established church,[3] but being almost entirely concentrated in one province they often had a very considerable local superiority and the moral strength which this brought. William King, who was bishop of Derry from 1691 to 1703, was an active enemy of the protestant dissenters; but he found them so strongly entrenched that any attempt to enforce the law strictly would have been unsuccessful and perhaps disastrous.[4] In preparation for his first visitation of the diocese he drew up articles to be enquired into by the churchwardens of each parish. The first article reads: 'Hath any in

[1] Stevenson, *Two centuries of life in Down*, pp. 171 ff.

[2] Sir Constantine Phipps to lord treasurer (Oxford), 26 Dec. 1712 (*Portland MSS*, v. 255).

[3] Sir William Petty, in the reign of Charles II, reckoned the churchmen and the protestant dissenters, apart from the Scots of the north, at 200,000, the Scots at 100,000 (*Political anatomy of Ireland* (1691), p. 8). Petty's estimate of the numbers of the 'English' non-conformists, whom he makes exactly equal to the 'legal protestants or conformists' may have been accurate in 1670, when it was made; but certainly before the end of the seventeenth century, protestant dissenters, other than presbyterians, had practically disappeared. It would, however, be impossible to estimate accurately the proportions absorbed by the other religious bodies.

[4] J. C. Beckett, 'William King's administration of the diocese of Derry', in *I.H.S.*, iv. 171 ff.

your parish traduced or spoken against the articles of religion ... or hath spoken or declared anything to the derogation or depraising the divine service contained in the *Book of common prayer* ... or hath condemned episcopal government ... ?' In the margin is the comment: 'These articles so far as they concern dissenters out of conscience are dispensed with'.[1] Thus the churchwardens might, with clear conscience, omit in their returns any reference to the protestant dissenters in their parishes, all of whom would probably be guilty of the whole catalogue of offences. There could hardly be a clearer indication that the dissenters could not be dealt with inside the existing ecclesiastical system. In the neighbouring diocese of Armagh the dissenters showed themselves strong enough even to take what they wanted by force, when they pulled down and carried off a meeting-house in Cookstown, and the law could do no more than fine forty of them sixpence apiece.[2] The wealth and efficiency of the presbyterian merchants formed the basis of their powerful influence in many Ulster towns,[3] but it was only towards the end of the eighteenth century that their influence became important in the political life of the kingdom as a whole. This delay was not due to repressive ecclesiastical legislation but to the fact that in eighteenth century Ireland, as in England at the same period, the exercise of political power was virtually confined to the landowning gentry and aristocracy. In Ireland it was the volunteer movement which gave an opening for the mercantile class to which most of the leaders of the presbyterians belonged. It was at least partly because of their new political importance that they were able to force a reluctant English government to give approval to the repeal of the test act, which was in fact rather a symbol of their legal inferiority than an effective check upon their power.

The exclusion of the protestant dissenters from direct political influence was not the main burden of their complaint during the eighteenth century. Their great grievance was that the sacramental test imposed in 1704 prevented their advancement in the public service. The answer of at least some of those who supported the test was that the number of protestant dissenters whose economic status made them eligible for any post of importance was very small. It is hard to believe that the test act made any serious difference. Throughout the eighteenth century the most profitable posts on the Irish establishment were

---

[1] 'Articles to be enquired into ... at the visitation of the bishop of Derry' (P.R.O.N.I., Ellis papers, no. 231).

[2] Bp King to Bp Lindsay of Killaloe, 23 Apr. 1702 (T.C.D., MS N.3. 2b, p. 19).

[3] J. C. Beckett, 'William King's administration of the diocese of Derry, 1691–1703', in *I.H.S.*, iv. 175.

reserved for Englishmen, and the rest were divided among the more influential Irish families and their supporters. Very few presbyterians were in a position to exercise the kind of influence necessary to secure such employments, even if there had been no test act to exclude them;[1] and that the act did in fact make very little difference in this connection is borne out by the absence of evidence that there was any general purging of the public service after its passage.[2] On the other hand, it is possible that some presbyterians may have held posts as deputies of the nominal officials, and in some parts of the north it would probably have been difficult to fill minor posts of merely local importance except by dissenters. It may have been on this account that a series of indemnity acts was passed from 1719 onwards until the final repeal of the test act, in so far as it affected protestant dissenters, in 1780.[3]

This survey of the economic status of the presbyterians in eighteenth century Ireland reinforces from another angle the arguments which have been put forward in the previous chapters. At first it might seem that, since the presbyterian community, consisting as it did of farmers and shopkeepers with a few squires and an increasing number of wealthy merchants, was almost automatically excluded from political power, there was no reason why it should arouse the jealousy of churchmen and landlords. But it was because the presbyterians refused to accept this exclusion that they were dangerous. Against the authority both of bishop and of civil magistrate they set up courts and exercised jurisdiction contrary to law. Their ecclesiastical connections with Scotland and their political alliance with the English whigs added to the strength which they drew from numbers, wealth and organisation. Irish landlords can hardly have failed to observe that it was in Ulster alone, where the presbyterians were most numerous, that tenant farmers enjoyed some sort of effective security of tenure. The Irish church welcomed and defended the sacramental test as a means of curbing a rival ecclesiastical organisation. By the Irish landlords it was regarded, during a great part of the eighteenth century, as a useful check upon the power of an emerging middle class. For both the church and the landlords it was a defensive weapon which may have delayed but could not finally prevent the success of their common enemy.

[1] Swift points out that Irish landlords found it impossible to make provision for their younger sons in the church, the law, the revenue, or the army, owing to the influx of Englishmen. Swift to the earl of Peterborough, 28 Apr. 1726 (*Swift correspondence*, iii. 310). There would not have been much room for the sons of presbyterian ministers, merchants and farmers.

[2] See Reid, *History*, ii. 512, and above, p. 49.

[3] See above, pp. 880–1.

CRITICAL NOTE ON AUTHORITIES

The shortness of the following list of authorities is some indication of the difficulties encountered in attempting to deal adequately with the subject. There is, certainly, plenty of information about the Irish presbyterians in the eighteenth century; but in order to trace their relations with the government it is necessary to have similar information about the government's policy and action. The history of the administration of Ireland in the eighteenth century, however, still requires much study and it is usually difficult and often impossible to discover just what the government intended in any particular instance, or even who was responsible for the measures proposed or carried out.

State papers provide the main sources of information about government action. The following have been used in the preparation of this work:

(a) *Calendar of state papers, domestic series, 1689–1704.*

(b) 'Transcripts of the state papers relating to Ireland' in the Public Record Office of Northern Ireland. This series, made under the direction of Dr D. A. Chart, deputy keeper of the records of Northern Ireland, begins in 1715 and now extends to 1743. It contains full transcripts of all documents relating to Northern Ireland and summaries of all documents relating to Ireland. It is arranged according to the order of the original documents (in the Public Record Office of England) which can be identified from the date-reference.

(c) *Calendar of home office papers, 1760–5.*

The data provided by all these collections is incomplete and unsatisfactory. Actions are recorded, but not the motives behind them; or when motives are suggested there is often an air of unreality about them, which leaves one with the impression that the true story lies beneath the surface. This appears very strongly in the accounts of the imposition of the sacramental test in 1703–4 and of the attempt to repeal it in 1731–3. From another point of view also these papers are unsatisfactory. The position of the presbyterians is considered only when the interest of the government is directly involved, so that the information which they yield gives very little indication of normal policy but only of the methods taken for dealing with particular problems. Nevertheless the first two sets of papers often provide a basis on which, with the help of other material, a reasonable and living representation of events can be built. The *Calendar of home office papers, 1760–75*, partly because the period concerned was one in which relations between the government and the presbyterians were in a stagnant condition, adds almost nothing either of fresh fact or of valuable illustration.

The presbyterian records, which form a natural complement to these documents, are the 'Minutes of the presbytery of Antrim', for the reign of James II, and *Records of the general synod of Ulster*, for the subsequent period. These provide a continuous outline, except for a brief gap at the beginning of William III's reign; but the outline is often very sketchy. This is quite natural. The synod met, in normal circumstances, once a year, and when it met it was more concerned with internal administration than with external relations. In spite of this it is disappointing to find so little information about the payment of *regium donum* and so little evidence about the operation of the sacramental test. The reason seems to be that these matters were left largely in the hands of committees; but even so, surprisingly little attention is given, in the synod's minutes, to the reports of these committees. The evidence of the *Records*, however, provides a valuable check on other sources of information. For instance the charge made against the presbyterians and denied by them that *regium donum* was used to aid in the setting up of new congregations can be proved from the minutes of the general synod.

To some extent the bare outline supplied by these official records is filled in by private and semi-official correspondence. *The state letters of Henry, earl of Clarendon* give a very clear picture of the condition of Ireland when the declaration of indulgence was issued. But few of the letters deal specially with the treatment or attitude of the presbyterians and such information as they give on the subject is merely incidental. The diary which is printed along with the letters gives some help in tracing the influence of Irish affairs during the confused period which followed William's arrival in England. Much more valuable material is available for the early eighteenth century. *The Correspondence of Robert Wodrow* deals primarily and almost exclusively with the presbyterians, and though mainly concerned with Scotland the references to Ireland are numerous and important. A great part of the Irish section of the correspondence is, however, taken up with internal problems and especially with the non-subscription controversy. On the other hand there is much useful information on the imposition and effect of the oath of abjuration. Apart from the actual facts which it yields this correspondence is an important illustration of the close relations maintained by the Irish presbyterians with their co-religionists in Scotland.

The correspondence of William King (who was successively dean of St. Patrick's, bishop of Derry and archbishop of Dublin) is even more useful. The following sources have been drawn on for King's letters:

(*a*) C. S. King, *A great archbishop of Dublin.*

(*b*) King correspondence in the library of Trinity College, Dublin.

(*c*) R. Mant, *History of the church of Ireland.*

(*d*) Royal Commission on Historical Manuscripts, *Second report.*

Wherever possible letters have been quoted from the printed sources, and though most of these have been checked from the manuscripts only one minor correction (noted where it occurs) has been necessary. Of the three printed sources the only satisfactory one is Mant, who used the letters at his disposal intelligently to illustrate his narrative. The Historical Manuscripts Commission report gives little more than a few samples of the correspondence, while C. S. King has printed a heterogeneous collection, interesting enough in itself, but chosen on no discernible principle. Taken as a whole, this correspondence throws light upon two important aspects of the subject. First, it shows the attitude of the established church to the presbyterians. Secondly, it shows the relations between church and state on the policy to be followed towards them. The value of the correspondence is greatly increased by the fact that it contains not only letters written by King but letters written to him, so that many different view-points are represented. *The correspondence of Jonathan Swift* and *The letters of Swift to Ford* supplement the information given by the King correspondence, but except on the controversy over the proposed repeal of the sacramental test in 1731–3 have little independent value in the present connection. Archbishop Boulter's *Letters* give useful information on two points only, emigration and the failure of the proposed repeal of the test in 1733.

Other correspondence of minor importance is to be found scattered through the reports of the Historical Manuscripts Commission. The volumes from which quotations have been made are given in the bibliography but none of them can be regarded as a main source for the history of Irish presbyterianism.

Along with these collections of letters may be mentioned the Crosslé papers (P.R.O.N.I.), a volume of transcripts of miscellaneous documents formerly in the Public Record Office of Ireland. The most important of these documents are letters, many of which bear directly on the position and treatment of the Irish presbyterians during the eighteenth century, especially on the fortunes of Alexander McCracken and his companions during the controversy over the abjuration oath. There are also some documents relating to *regium donum* and some letters on the Belturbet affair of 1712.

The pamphlet literature is plentiful but for the present purpose almost useless. The same arguments on each side are repeated without material variation, while very little is said which helps to explain the real reason for the policy of the government and the attitude of the established church. Two pamphlets may be singled out, partly as representative of the general mass in the main arguments which they use, partly because they do more than merely reiterate the words of their predecessors. These are, first, *The conduct of the dissenters of Ireland* and secondly, *An historical essay upon the loyalty of presbyterians*. The first of these, usually attributed to William Tisdal,[1] gives a good deal of valuable information about the state of affairs in the north of Ireland during the reigns of William III and of Anne and indicates quite clearly, with concrete examples, why the churchmen feared the presbyterians. The second, a solid volume of between five and six hundred pages, not only advances all the arguments usually employed on behalf of the presbyterians but, as its title suggests, provides useful historical information, including a number of letters and other documents. The pamphlets of Dean Swift have not the same historical value, but they are interesting in themselves and they serve as a reminder that the issues at stake, however trifling they may seem today, were taken seriously by one whose intellectual outlook was much wider than that of most of his generation.

Secondary authorities fall into two groups, civil and ecclesiastical. The civil historians, Bagwell, Froude and Lecky, though they did not entirely ignore the problem to be faced, made little headway towards solving it. Bagwell, indeed, was hardly concerned with the period under review. Both Froude and Lecky, on the other hand, dealt directly with the eighteenth century and both considered specifically the position and treatment of the presbyterians. But neither of them produced a reasonable explanation of the government's policy nor of the part played by the established church in having that policy carried out. The reason for this was not lack of information but lack of perception. Froude had in mind a fixed idea of what government policy ought to have been and by this standard he judged every action without weighing the arguments on the other side. Lecky's attitude was more nearly impartial but in effect his conclusion was the same. Though both dealt with the position and treatment of the presbyterians neither of them gave the matter very much space. Froude's brevity arose from his belief that when he had attributed the treatment of the presbyterians to the folly of the government and the bigotry of the churchmen he had solved every problem connected with it. Lecky might have dealt with the matter more fully but for the fact that his real interest was with the last two decades of the century, by which time the presbyterian controversy had fallen into the background.

[1] Vicar of Belfast, *c.* 1716–36 (Benn, *History of Belfast*, pp. 382 ff.).

Naturally ecclesiastical historians have had more to say. Mant, in his *History of the church of Ireland*, did deal with the attitude of the established church towards the presbyterians and did say something of the effect of this attitude on government policy. But he made no attempt at a critical analysis of the facts and satisfied himself with repeating the arguments used by eighteenth-century churchmen. The chief value of his work lies in the use he made of Archbishop King's letters. Killen, though he added little to the subject in his own *Ecclesiastical history of Ireland*, did valuable work by completing and editing Reid's *History of the presbyterian church in Ireland*. This, in spite of some faults of partisanship, remains without a rival. But even Reid did not see the true nature of the problem which confronted him, and his explanation of the policy of the government towards the presbyterians and of the attitude of the churchmen is not at all convincing. However, if his judgment was sometimes at fault his facts seldom require correction. On one point indeed, through oversight or partisanship, he fell into error. The presbyterians were frequently accused of using *regium donum* to establish new congregations and for political purposes. This they denied and Reid accepted the denial at its face value (*History*, iii. 21). But the minutes of the general synod, of which he elsewhere made considerable use, show that both charges had some foundation. This, however, is a small point, and in general Reid carried out his task so thoroughly that any study of Irish presbyterianism (this work included) must be little more than a commentary on his *History*.

Two other books must be mentioned. Irwin's *History of presbyterianism in Dublin and the south and west of Ireland* deals fairly fully with an aspect of presbyterian history which has otherwise been scarcely touched on in any published work. The main point on which the author seems to be in error (the *regium donum*) is referred to in a note at the end of chapter X. Witherow's *Historical and literary memorials of presbyterianism in Ireland* is of more importance. It is really a sort of guide to all the books published by Irish presbyterians during the eighteenth century, and though it may be incomplete its value to the historian can be easily realised, for it contains not only notes on the lives of the writers and lists of their publications but also copious extracts, which are all the more welcome since the originals are often difficult to obtain.

BIBLIOGRAPHY

A. UNPRINTED SOURCES

I. *Public Record Office of Northern Ireland, Belfast*
Transcripts of the State Papers relating to Ireland, 1715–43.
Transcript of 'Payment and receipt book, revenue and army, Ireland, June 1690–March 1691' (T.689).
Crosslé Papers (T.780).
Transcript of Wodrow Papers in National Library of Scotland (T.525).
Ellis papers.

II. *Library of Trinity College, Dublin*
Correspondence of William King:
  (i) original letters to and from King;
  (ii) letter-books containing copies of letters from King;
  (iii) transcripts of letters from King (including some in the Public Library, Armagh) made by E. A. Phelps, late assistant librarian, T.C.D.

III. *Marsh's Library, Dublin*
Correspondence between the lords justices and the bishop of Down, concerning the appointment of churchwardens (MS. Z. 3. 1. 1. xiii).

IV. *In the library of the Presbyterian Historical Society, Belfast*
Transcript of the minutes of the presbytery of Antrim during the reign of James II.

V. *In private hands*
Palatine papers: transcripts of documents (formerly in P.R.O.I.) relating to the settlement of the palatine protestants in Ireland, made by George Shummacher, Esq., formerly of P.R.O.I. and now in his possession.

B. PRINTED SOURCES

I. DOCUMENTARY COLLECTIONS
Calendar of state papers, domestic series, 1689–1704, 13 vols, 1895–1924.
Calendar of home office papers, 1760–75, 4 vols, 1878–99.
Constitutions and canons ecclesiastical, Dublin, 1714.

Publications of the Historical Manuscripts Commission:
Buccleuch and Queensberry MSS, 3 vols, 1897–9.
Buckinghamshire MSS (*rep. 14*, app. ix), 1895.

150

BIBLIOGRAPHY

Charlemont MSS, i, 1894.
Downshire MSS, i, 1924.
Finch MSS, 2 vols, 1913, 1922.
House of lords MSS, new series, v, 1910.
Laing MSS, ii, 1925.
Lothian MSS, 1908.
Portland MSS, iv. 1897; v, 1899.
Second report (King correspondence), 1871.
Stopford-Sackville MSS, 2 vols, 1904, 1910.
Stuart papers, ii, 1904.
Various collections, vi (MSS of Miss Eyre Matcham and additional MSS of Capt. H. V. Knox), 1909.
Westmoreland MSS, 1885.

Journals of the house of commons of Ireland, Dublin, 1781.
Journals of the house of lords of Ireland, Dublin, 1779.
Liber Munerum Publicorum Hiberniae, 2 vols, London, 1852.
Records of the general synod of Ulster, 3 vols, Belfast, 1890, 1897, 1898.
Statutes at large of England and of Great Britain, 10 vols, London, 1811.
Statutes at large passed in the parliaments held in Ireland, 13 vols, Dublin, 1786.
Thirtieth report of the Deputy Keeper of the Public Records ... in Ireland, Dublin, 1899.
Tudor and Stuart proclamations, calendared by Robert Steele under the direction of the earl of Crawford, 2 vols, Oxford, 1910.

II. Correspondence

Analecta Hibernica, i. 38–9 (Tyrconnell to lord president, 9 May 1688, Bodl. Rawl. A. 139 b. f. 108).
Correspondence of Jonathan Swift, ed. F. E. Ball, 6 vols, London, 1910–14.
Correspondence of Robert Wodrow, ed. T. McCrie, 3 vols, Edinburgh, 1842–3.
King, C. S. (ed.), *A great archbishop of Dublin; William King, 1650–1729, his autobiography, family, and a selection from his correspondence*, London, 1906.
Letters written by ... Hugh Boulter, D.D., lord primate of all Ireland, 2 vols, Oxford, 1769–70.
Letters of Jonathan Swift to Charles Ford, ed. D. Nichol Smith, Oxford, 1935.

151

BIBLIOGRAPHY

State letters of Henry, earl of Clarendon, lord lieutenant of Ireland during the reign of King James II, and his lordship's diary for the years 1687, 1688, 1689 and 1690, 2 vols, Oxford and Dublin, 1765.

III. CONTEMPORARY AND NEARLY CONTEMPORARY WORKS

Abernethy, J., *The nature and consequence of the sacramental test considered,* Dublin, 1731 ; in *Tracts and sermons,* London, 1751.

Answer to A vindication of marriage as solemnized by presbyterians in the north of Ireland, 1704.

Burdy, S., *Life of Skelton,* Dublin, 1792, ed. N. Moore, Oxford, 1914.

Burnet, G., *History of his own time,* 4 vols, 1753.

Calamy, E., *An historical account of my own life, with some reflections on the times I have lived in (1671–1731),* ed. J. T. Rutt, 2 vols, London, 1829.

Conduct of the dissenters of Ireland with respect both to church and state, Dublin, 1712.

Cox, R., *Autobiography of Sir Richard Cox,* ed. R. Caulfield, London and Cork, 1860.

Crawford, W., *History of Ireland,* 2 vols, Strabane, 1783.

Edmundson, W., *Journal of his life and work,* Dublin, 1715.

Hamilton, A., *A true relation of the actions of the Inniskilling men,* 1690.

Hamilton, J., *The Hamilton manuscripts,* ed. T. K. Lowry, Belfast, 1876.

Hamilton, W., *Life and character of James Bonnell,* London, 1707.

[Kennedy, G. (jr.)], *The great blessing of peace and truth in our days,* Belfast, 1749.

King, W., *An answer to the considerations which compelled Peter Manby, as he pretends, to embrace what he calls the catholic religion,* 1687.

King, W., *State of the protestants of Ireland under King James's government,* 1691.

[Kirkpatrick, J.], *Historical essay upon the loyalty of presbyterians,* [Belfast], 1713.

McBride, J., *A sermon before the provincial synod at Antrim, preached June 1, 1698,* Belfast, 1698.

McKenzie, J., *A narrative of the siege of Londonderry,* London, 1690; ed. W. D. Killen, Belfast, 1861.

Narrative of the proceedings of seven general synods of the northern presbyterians in Ireland, with relation to their differences, 1720–6, Belfast, 1727.

Petty, W., *Political anatomy of Ireland,* London, 1691.

BIBLIOGRAPHY

Swift, J., *The advantages proposed by repealing the sacramental test, impartially considered*, London, 1732.[1]

Swift, J., *The presbyterians' plea of merit*, Dublin, 1733.[1]

Swift, J., *A narrative of the several attempts which the dissenters of Ireland have made, for a repeal of the sacramental test*, Dublin, 1733.[1]

Swift, J., *Queries wrote by Dr J. Swift, in the year 1732*, Dublin, 1733.[1]

Synge, E., *A defence of the established church and laws in answer to a book entitled A vindication of marriage as solemnized by the presbyterians in the north of Ireland*, 1705.

A vindication of marriage as solemnized by presbyterians in the north of Ireland, 1702.

Walker, G., *A true account of the siege of Londonderry*, London, 1689.

Ware, J., *Writers of Ireland*, in *Works*, ed. W. Harris, ii, Dublin, 1745.

Wesley, J., *Journal of the Rev. John Wesley*, ed. N. Curnock, 8 vols, London, 1909–16.

Wodrow, R., *Analecta, materials for a history of remarkable providences, mostly relating to Scotch ministers and Christians*, 4 vols, Edinburgh, 1842–3.

C. LATER WORKS

Armstrong, J., *History of the presbyterian churches in the city of Dublin*, Dublin, 1829.

Bagwell, R., *Ireland under the Stuarts*, iii, London, 1916.

Beckett, J. C., 'The government and the church of Ireland under William III and Anne', in *I.H.S.*, ii. 280–302 (1941).

Beckett, J. C., 'William King's administration of the diocese of Derry, 1691–1703', in *I.H.S.*, iv. 164–80 (1944).

Benn, G., *History of Belfast*, London, 1877.

Bigger, F. J., *The Ulster land war of 1770*, Dublin, 1910.

Black, R., *Substance of two speeches delivered in the general synod of Ulster, 1812*, Dublin, n.d.

Cambridge Modern History, vols v–vi, Cambridge, 1908–9.

Carré, A., *L'influence des huguenots français en Irelande aux xviie et xviiie siècles*, Paris, 1937.

Crookshank, C. H., *History of methodism in Ireland*, 3 vols, Belfast, 1885–8.

Ford, H. J., *The Scotch-Irish in America*, Princeton, 1915.

Forster, J., *Life of Jonathan Swift 1667–1711*, London, 1875.

[1] All these are quoted from *Prose works of Jonathan Swift*, ed. T. Scott, iv, London, 1898.

BIBLIOGRAPHY

Froude, J. A., *The English in Ireland in the eighteenth century*, 3 vols, London, 1887.

Irwin, C. H., *History of presbyterianism in Dublin and the south and west of Ireland*, London, 1890.

Killen, W. D., *Ecclesiastical history of Ireland*, 2 vols, London, 1875.

Killen, W. D. (ed.), *History of the congregations of the presbyterian church in Ireland*, Belfast, 1886.

Lecky, W. E. H., *History of Ireland in the eighteenth century*, 5 vols, London, 1892.

Lee, G. L., *Huguenot settlements in Ireland*, London, 1936.

Life and times of Selina, countess of Huntingdon, 2 vols, London, 1839.

Mant, R., *History of the church of Ireland from the revolution to the union of the churches of England and Ireland*, London, 1840.

Mathews, G., *Account of the regium donum issued to the presbyterian church of Ireland*, Dublin, 1836.

McCracken, J. L., 'The conflict between the Irish administration and parliament, 1753–6', in *I.H.S.*, iii. 159–79.

McDowell, R. B., *Irish public opinion, 1750–1800*, London, 1944.

Memoirs of a huguenot family translated and compiled from the original autobiography of the reverend James Fontaine, London, n.d.

Phillips, A. (ed.), *History of the church of Ireland*, 3 vols, Oxford, 1933–4.

Pike, Clement E., 'The origin of the *regium donum*', in *Transactions of Royal Historical Society*, third series, iii (1909).

Political Christianity, London, 1834.

Reid, J. S., *History of the presbyterian church in Ireland*, ed. W. D. Killen, 3 vols, Belfast, 1867.

Report of the Presbyterian Historical Society of Ireland, 1909, Belfast, 1909.

Stevenson, J., *Two centuries of life in Down*, Belfast, 1920.

Wight, T. and Rutty, J., *History of the rise and progress of the people called quakers in Ireland*, London, 1811.

Witherow, T., *Historical and literary memorials of presbyterianism in Ireland*, 2 vols, Belfast, 1879–80.

INDEX

The names of modern historians are asterisked.

INDEX

Schoolmasters, licensing of, 29, 40–1

Schools, presbyterian, 89

Scotland, Ulster presbyterians and, 14, 17, 23, 28, 35, 38, 66, 67, 99, 144, 146; 22, 114

Scots, Ulster, 14, 20, 34, 38

Seceders, 99 and *n*.

Seymour, Sir Edward, 38

Shrewsbury, Charles Talbot, 12th earl and 1st duke of, and the Irish presbyterians, 33; succeeds Ormond as lord lieutenant, 60 and *n*.

Silesia, protestants in, 51; protestant refugees from, 130

Skelton, Philip, 99, 102

Smith, Edward, bp of Down, 121

Smith, Samuel, 120

South of Ireland, protestant dissenters of: petition against sacramental test, 87, 90; relations with synod of Ulster, 98–9; and *regium donum*, 106, 111–2, 115; *see* Dublin

Southwell, Sir Robert, and *regium donum*, 29, 107, 111; and sacramental test, 44, 52; 27, 41, 45, 50, 51, 119

Spain, 75

Spencer, Brent, 68, 69

Stanhope, James Stanhope, 1st earl, 76

Statutes:
2 Eliz. c. 2 (Ir.), *see* Uniformity, act of

17 & 18 Chas II c. 6 (Ir.), *see* Uniformity, act of

25 Chas II c. 12 (Eng.), 31, 46, 49

3 Wm & Mary c. 2 (Eng.), 18, 29, 40 and *n*., 132 *n*.

4 Wm & Mary c. 2 (Ir.), 125, 128

13 & 14 Wm III c. 6 (Eng.), *see* Abjuration, oath of

1 Anne 2 c. 17 (Eng.), *see* Abjuration, oath of

2 Anne c. 6 (Ir.), *see* Sacramental test

2 Anne c. 14 (Ir.), 128

2 Geo. I c. 9 (Ir.), 133

4 Geo. I c. 9 (Ir.), 128

5 Geo. I c. 4 (Eng.), 76 *n*.

6 Geo. I c. 5 (Ir.), *see* Toleration act

6 Geo. I c. 9 (Ir.), *see* Indemnity acts

10 Geo. I c. 8 (Ir.), 84 and *n*., 134 and *n*.

1 Geo. II c. 5 (Ir.), 134

9 Geo. II c. 16 (Ir.), 134

11 Geo. II c. 10 (Ir.), 122

19 Geo. II c. 18 (Ir.), 134

29 Geo. II c. 24 (Ir.), 84

19 & 20 Geo. III c. 6 (Ir.), *see* Sacramental test, repeal of

21 & 22 Geo. III c. 25 (Ir.), 122

7 & 8 Vic. c. 81, 122

See pp. 81–2

Stewart, Robert, afterwards Viscount Castlereagh and 2nd marquis of Londonderry, 140

Stipends of presbyterian ministers, 29, 111, 112, 114

Stirling, Thomas, presbyterian nonjuror, 66

Strabane, 36, 113

Sunderland, Charles Spencer, 3rd earl of, 76, 115

Supremacy, oath of, abrogated in Ireland, 29; 34, 40

Sweden, 75

Swift, Jonathan, dean of St Patrick's, and the sacramental test, 16 and *n*.; 45, 47, 92–3; 48, 88, 94, 147, 148

Switzerland, 125

Sydney, Henry Sydney, 1st Viscount, afterwards 1st earl of Romney, lord lieutenant, 32, 36

Synge, Edward, successively bp of Raphoe and abp of Tuam, 119 *n*., 121

Synod of Ulster: and presbyterian schoolmasters, 40–1; and presbyterian marriages, 41, 59, 117, 118, 120, 121; and abjuration oath, 65, 67; and non-subscribers, 83 *n*., 98, 99, 112, 113; and presbytery of Dublin, 98; and *regium donum*, 108–9, 113, 114, 149; 86, 87, 91 *n*., 97, 99 *n*., 124, 146

Templepatrick, 23

Thirty-nine articles, 75, 78

Tisdal, William, vicar of Belfast, 58, 148 and *n*.; see *Conduct of the dissenters*

Tithes: presbyterians and, 28, 89, 114; quakers and, 132, 133, 134, 135; 38, 78, 88, 97, 100

Toleration, presbyterian struggle for, 28, 29, 31–9, 71–7; 40, 45, 49

Toleration act (1719), 77–8, 83, 114

Tories: in power in England, 53, 104,

160